THE PASSOVER SEDER

THE
PASSOVER
SEDER

RUTH GRUBER FREDMAN

A MERIDIAN BOOK
NEW AMERICAN LIBRARY
TIMES MIRROR
NEW YORK AND SCARBOROUGH, ONTARIO

296.4
F

Published by arrangement with University of Pennsylvania Press

 MERIDIAN TRADEMARK REG. U.S. PAT. OFF. AND FOREIGN COUNTRIES
REGISTERED TRADEMARK—MARCA REGISTRADA
HECHO EN WESTFORD, MASS., U.S.A.

SIGNET, SIGNET CLASSICS, MENTOR, PLUME,
MERIDIAN and NAL BOOKS are published *in the
United States* by The New American Library, Inc.,
1633 Broadway, New York, New York 10019, *in Canada*
by The New American Library of Canada Limited, 81
Mack Avenue, Scarborough, Ontario M1L 1M8

Library of Congress Cataloging in Publication Data

Fredman, Ruth Gruber, 1934–
  The Passover Seder
  Reprint. Originally published: Philadelphia :
University of Pennsylvania, 1981. (Symbol and culture)
  Bibliography: p.
  Includes index.
  1. Seder. 2. Judaism—Liturgy—Texts—History and
criticism. 3. Haggadah. 4. Haggadot. 5. Seder—
Liturgy—Texts—History and criticism. I. Title.
II. Series: Symbol and culture.
[BM695.P35F73 1983]   296.4′37   82–18853
ISBN 0–452–00606–6

First Meridian Printing, April, 1983

1 2 3 4 5 6 7 8 9
PRINTED IN THE UNITED STATES OF AMERICA

2147

To Lauren, Andrew, Jonathan, and Florence

Contents

Preface

Abdul Hamid M. el-Zein, my teacher and my friend, was to have written the preface to this book. His words would have honored the work, but Zein died suddenly in August 1979, and has returned to his native Alexandria.

In Zein the rationalist and the mystic were combined: like many scientists, he sought an essential unity in the universe underlying the multiplicity of social experience. In his last article, Zein acknowledged the widely accepted position in anthropology that "man does order his world through systems of meaning," and continued "the problem now is to find a means of understanding that order which reaches the desired level of universality without diluting or destroying the significance of this diversity and the richness of meaning in human experience" (1977: 250). It was this endeavor which led Zein to structuralism as a system that extends beyond the particular historical configuration that is called a culture, and is implicit in all social thought and thus in the products of social thought—kinship systems, economic patterns, language, ritual, and mythology.

Zein saw anthropology as the supreme humanistic endeavor, as well as a science attempting to answer the fundamental questions about the nature of mankind. Anthropology meant learning about other societies and, by reflection, about our own, with the ultimate—one might say utopian—goal of making the strange familiar and so robbing it of its capacity to threaten. As he saw it, this is the most scholars might do: as they make the exotic intelligible and help us to understand ourselves, they coax the world a bit closer to empathy and to peace.

It was Zein, the Egyptian, who first suggested this project, noting the similarity of the items used in the Seder to objects used in ritual and in daily life throughout North Africa and the Middle East, and the unique use to which these common forms are put in Jewish culture. His influence on this study is profound and appreciated.

Zein lived what he believed. His sheer joy in learning, his delight in grappling with thought, his warmth, his humor, and his belief in his work inspired and enriched all of us who had the pleasure of knowing him.

With love and respect

Acknowledgments

The study of a social text such as the Seder requires the cooperation of many individuals and the examination of many literary works. While I have used multiple written sources, which I cite, it has also been through repeated personal observation of the ritual and through conversations with scholars and participants that the picture of the Seder presented on the following pages has been developed.

The works on Jewish subjects are exhaustive. Since a society's culture in its broadest sense is any manifestation of social or mental activity, I have consulted books and recorded oral information on custom, law, superstition, belief, folk sayings, and literature. Since in daily life people do not abstract and discriminate between ideas that influence their actions, I have considered recollection and actual practice, and the more ideal prescriptions of the Law, as equally informative.

There is one person who has been especially important in directing me to the fundamental written sources, and in clarifying practices and concepts in the broadest range of Jewish culture. I am deeply grateful to Rabbi Yaacov Lieberman, ritual director of Beth Sholom Congregation, Elkins Park, Pennsylvania, for hours of discussion in the early stages of this project. I was extremely fortunate to have someone so knowledgeable, so accommodating, and so good-natured and encouraging to assist me.

There are many others, too numerous to name individually, to whom I am indebted for their time, knowledge, and insight. Of course, the synthesis of all the bits and pieces of information so gathered—my analysis—is totally my responsibility.

Several persons have worked with me in developing the argument of this book and have offered invaluable criticism. Abdul Hamid M. el-Zein and Henry Selby reviewed the original draft, and J. David Sapir and Marc Schloss have given me very helpful comments on the later version. Above all, I wish to thank Michelle Zimbalist Rosaldo, whose editorial skill, perception, and suggestions have provided crucial guidance in producing the final form of this work.

I have been fortunate also in having the support and cooperation of my husband and my children throughout this endeavor. Their interest and encouragement have eased the way considerably for me. They have often provided the first forum of discussion and reflection for many of the ideas; in fact, the questions about Jewish ritual and social practice that occurred to these handy informants have often stimulated further inquiry on my part.

Introduction

The culture of a people is an ensemble of
texts, themselves ensembles, which the
anthropologist strains to read over the shoulders of
those to whom they properly belong . . .

    . . . art forms generate and regenerate the very
subjectivity they pretend only to display.
                Clifford Geertz
                Deep Play: Notes on the
                Balinese Cockfight

Each spring, throughout the world, Jews gather in small
family or community groups to observe a ritual two thousand years old
—the Seder of Passover. The Seder celebrated today has been developed from practices begun thousands of years ago. The ritual of Passover, past and present, has provided a formal, relatively concise forum
for the expression of the ideas and experiences of Jewish society, a time
and place for reflection, questioning, and reaffirmation.

Before proceeding to the analysis of the Seder itself, a few comments are in order about the general nature of the society that has
created and celebrated the Seder, about the perspective of the author,
and about the manner in which the material for this study has been
gathered.

The term "Jewish society" masks an enormous internal diversity of
faith, practice, knowledge, teachings, and commitment. Yet one idea is
fundamental to the culture. Despite the great emphasis on knowledge,
"not learning but doing is the chief thing," as the Talmud says (Sayings
of the Fathers, 1:17).[1] The Talmud is the exhaustive commentary on the

---

1. This section of the Talmud, *Pirke Avot,* is more commonly called Ethics of the
Fathers. I use the title given by Joseph Hertz, from whose translation this quotation is
taken.

Torah, or Law; these books are the society's most important texts. The Torah provides the standard for the conduct of one's life; it is understood by the most pious as the word of God and the story of the creation of the earth, of humanity, and of the Jews as a people. The Torah is the first of the three parts of the Hebrew Bible, collectively known as the Tanakh; it consists of the "Five Books of Moses": Genesis, Exodus, Leviticus, Numbers, and Deuteronomy. The second part is the writings of the Prophets. The third, known as Hagiographia, or Sacred Writings, consists of eleven books, including Psalms, Proverbs, and the Song of Songs. Quotations from the Tanakh in this study are from the editions published by the Jewish Publication Society, the *Holy Scriptures,* 1917 translation (1947 printing), or the newer 1962 translation of the first five books, the *Torah.*

The Talmud is minute exegesis of the Torah and provides the model for all attempts to make the eternal standard practical in all historical circumstances. Throughout the Talmud the emphasis is on man's deeds, not his unfulfilled intentions or academic accomplishments. "He whose deeds exceed his wisdom, his wisdom shall endure; but he whose wisdom exceeds his deeds, his wisdom shall not endure" (Sayings of the Fathers, 3:12). Deeds are "informed action," the place where ideal prescriptions are realized in social context. In Judaism the word *mitzvah* ("commandment") has come to mean the uniting of heaven and earth through man's conscious action, whether by following the 613 explicit commands of the Torah, or by performing any action that expresses one's compassion or obligation toward other men.

If a goal of life is the recognition of every opportunity to perform a *mitzvah,* it is extremely important to comprehend God's will as completely as possible. A great body of interpretive writings has developed about the Torah in order to make God's will intelligible and practical. Principal among these works is the Talmud (both "learning" and "teachings"). There are actually two Talmuds, one written in Palestine and completed about 300 or 400 C.E. and the other written in Babylonia and completed about a century later. The Babylonian Talmud is much larger than the Palestinian and has received much more intensive study. References to the Talmud throughout this work are to the Babylonian Talmud, unless otherwise indicated by "T.J.," or "Jerusalem Talmud," preceding the citation.

The Talmud is divided into two main sections: the Mishnah (from the root "to repeat," also indicating "to teach") and the Gemara ("completion" or "perfection" of knowledge).[2] These authoritative commentaries are part of each page of the Talmud. There is also a vast corpus of rabbinic interpretations known as Midrash ("investigation"), which further extend and reconstruct the meanings of the Torah. The Midrash, like much of the Gemara, includes legend, maxim, and folk practice. Collectively, this nonlegalistic lore is known as Aggadah or Haggadah.

In the Middle Ages, several attempts were made to present the laws in a way that would make them more easily accessible in daily life. In 1180 Maimonides' *Mishneh Torah* appeared; in the fourteenth century, Rabbi Jacob Ben Asher's *Tur;* and soon afterward, the Code of Jewish Law (or *Shulhan Arukh,* "set table") of Rabbi Joseph Caro. All of these works contain maxims and advice for the conduct of daily life, as well as providing a code for living and explicating the details of ritual actions. Caro's four-volume work, as adjusted for populations in Europe in the sixteenth century by Rabbi Moses Isserles of Poland, is still widely influential, and was made more concise and even more accessible through its abridgment into one volume, the *Kitzer Shulhan Arukh,* by Rabbi Solomon Ganzfried in the nineteenth century. Throughout this study, references to the Code of Jewish Law are to Ganzfried's edition.

The process of interpreting the Law and making it practical for everyday life continues to the present day. In ancient times, legal questions were sent to learned rabbis in Babylonia, and the answers, the *Responsa,* were collected and studied; eminent rabbis today are still asked their opinions on how the Torah can be made consistent with modern life, and these opinions are circulated and debated.

The rabbis who compiled the Talmud and the many other commentaries, and those who continue in their tradition today, treat all areas of experience as interwoven and contributory to the fabric of everyday life. Unlike many contemporary writers on Jewish culture, who separate their subject into collections of folk sayings and folk customs, magical practices, historical events, ritual precepts and such, the

2. The Jews living in Babylonia and Palestine created a vast amount of Oral Law, exegesis of the Torah, which could not be written down lest it appear to be either an addition to the divine Torah or a competitor to it, but which was necessary in order to relate the Law to their existence. This Oral Law was taught through repetition and open discussion. This body of material eventually became too voluminous for any memory, and, in order to save it, it was finally committed to writing. However, as soon as it was written down, the need was felt for further amplification of the Oral Law, which resulted in the Gemara. The Mishnah was created to complement the Torah, and the Gemara in turn became an expansion of the Mishnah.

writers of the Talmud mixed together all these aspects of daily life in their work and considered each of them in their deliberations, in keeping with the idea that "a custom in Israel is as valid as the Law" (Code of Jewish Law, vol. 1, 44:4). Today, the question of whether or not one is permitted to drive to the synagogue on the Sabbath involves a consideration of present-day living arrangements in contrast to those during biblical and talmudic times, the meanings of "Sabbath" and "work," the application of "work" to mechanical devices unknown to talmudic experience, and the relative merits of upholding the biblical concept of the Sabbath as compared with the need for community assembly, also an imperative in Judaism. And, in keeping with the diversity of individual and group experience in Judaism, there is no one resolution accepted by all groups as the definitive expression of the intent of God's word.

In the Talmud, the emphasis is always on the here-and-now, not on heaven or the hereafter. There is never any separation into "ideal" and "real" worlds, and although the compilers of the Talmud accepted and dealt with a whole world of intangible beings—good and evil impulses, demons, angels, the powers inherent in numbers—this world is only sketched in and then discussed in terms of its influence on man's ability to act in accordance with the will of God.

God himself is only briefly sketched in Jewish thought. The Torah and Talmud are not theo-logy, nor are any subsequent writings. The twelfth-century philosopher Maimonides delineated the argument once and for all: God is accepted as omniscient and omnipotent, just, merciful, and loving, but is ultimately beyond description by man. God is so distinct from man that even the terms man uses to describe God must be understood in the negative: to say that God is "just" merely means he is not unjust as the term is understood among men; it is not a positive definition of a knowable attribute. Any attempt to impose man's descriptive terms on God diminishes him and makes him appear an exalted man rather than a different sort of entity altogether. Although a person may hope to comprehend God's will through his words, such comprehension is necessarily compromised by man's mental limitations and by the meanings current in his social context. Maimonides' argument therefore considers the symbolic nature of language and the limitations of words in apprehending absolute reality, whether this reality is understood as God or as depersonalized causation.

Jewish eschatology, like "God," remains underdeveloped, especially when compared with the highly elaborated treatment of how people should conduct their lives on earth. There are discussions of a messianic time to come, which will be characterized by mankind's triumph over sin and the return of the Jews to their ancient land, and by life in the World to Come, *Olam HaBa,* which will be a state of peace and plenty, but the place of this golden dream is the earth, not heaven.

As God's creation, the earth and all its pleasures are good and to be enjoyed, as in Psalm 24:1, "The earth is the Lord's and the fullness thereof. . . ." The pious Jew says a blessing on encountering a wonder of nature new to him—an ocean, a rainbow—and when performing any new act which brings him joy, whether eating a fruit for the first time in a new season or putting on a new garment. The Talmud warns that "a man is to give account in the Hereafter for any permissible pleasures from which he abstained" (T.J. Kiddushin, 4:12), and that the habitual faster is a sinner (Taanith, 11a). The question for the Jew is not one of escaping the earth or his God-created body, but of acting in such a manner that he brings heaven to earth. Such union of heaven and earth in daily life hastens the coming of the messiah, and is a foretaste of the World to Come. But man need not, should not, wait for such a distant occurrence. "If you are planting a tree and you hear that the Messiah has come, first finish planting and then run to the city gates and tell him Shalom," is an often repeated saying of the first-century scholar Yochanan ben Zakkai.

The role of the symbolic as practical action can best be seen in the case of the Hasidim, the "fervent" or "pious" groups of Jews who practice what is often called "mystical Judaism." The Hasidim have continued, and made "practical," the teachings collectively known as the Kabbala (received oral "tradition"), mystic speculations on the origin and profound significance of the universe, the essence of the Supreme Being, and the destiny of man which originated in Babylonia in the sixth century B.C.E. Until the Middle Ages, the Kabbala was studied and transmitted by a rather small circle of rabbinic mystics, but in about the fourteenth century, and especially after the expulsion of the Jews from Spain in 1492, kabbalism became a means through which the messianic hopes and yearnings of the Jews in Europe found a voice. A series of kabbalistic treatises, coming from centers in Safed, Israel and in Europe from about 1550 to 1750, popularized kabbalistic thought and changed it from a privileged esoteric discipline into an aid to comprehension of the conditions of existence outside Israel.

Hasidism has continued in this tradition, adding its own writings, and concerning itself less with the metaphysical and theosophical as-

pect of the Kabbala than with the way each individual might act morally to bring union with God. Rabbi Schneur Zalman of Liadi, the
founder of the more psychological and philosophical school of Hasidism,
Habad, compared the mystic teachings of the Kabbala to salt, which
adds flavor to food though it is not a food itself (Birnbaum 1975:534). It
is estimated that by the nineteenth century at least half the Jews of the
world could be counted as adherents of Hasidism (Ausubel 1964:87).

The images and explorations of the Kabbala influenced thought
among populations that did not accept the teachings as such. This was
possible because many kabbalistic concepts, although fanciful, have
their roots in the Torah and the Talmud and are not specifically contrary to the Law.

Because of their interest in mysticism's highly elaborated accounts
of creation, the nature of good and evil, and the soul, it would seem that
the Hasidim dwell in an esoteric universe of divine emanations, "animal
souls," and multiple worlds marking the distance between man and
God. And yet this is not so. Union with God is never a private matter
but a collective endeavor; the Hasid hopes to raise the whole society to
a state of oneness with God, not just himself. Mysticism is, as it were,
socialized in Judaism. The mystic accepts the fundamental constructs
of society—its Law and its assumptions about the nature of God and the
material universe—and expands or improvises upon them to reach his
goal.

Instead of providing a means of escaping earthly existence, Hasidic
readings act as a further dimension to the comprehension of each person's role on earth, an expansion of information leading to action. The
more a man understands of the nature and purposes of God's design,
the better he can act to overcome evil in the world, rescue the good,
and so bring the messiah. It is the man who is part of this world and so
aware of temptation, the *benoni* or intermediate man, the man placed
between good and evil, who is the concern of the Habad school of
Hasidism. The arena in which the *benoni* can demonstrate his free will
and understanding of God's plan through his struggle against evil is the
society in which he lives. Consequently, the Hasid may not withdraw
from temptation or deny the pleasures of God's earth, whether food,
furnishings, or sex, as that would remove him from the fray. Abstinence
is as much a sin as overindulgence. The aim is balance, mastery, control.

Hasidism, therefore, has produced no contemplative orders and
prohibits mortification of the flesh as an insult to God's creation, and this
idea is found throughout Judaism. The Hasid follows the general Jewish

precept that a man must see that his son learns a trade, just as he ensures the child's religious education, in order that the child may someday be self-supporting. "Anyone who does not teach his son a skill or profession may be regarded as if he is teaching him to rob" (Talmud, Kiddushin, 29a), and the Talmud also advises a father to teach his son to swim, again so that the boy can take care of himself. The highest form of charity in Judaism is to provide the means through which a man may earn his own way. Most Hasidim are small artisans, tradesmen, or teachers, and even the leader of the community, the man believed to have achieved the greatest mastery over his "evil side," the *tzaddik* ("righteous") is involved in the daily, practical decisions of his people.

The symbolic world in Judaism is never a rarified realm but a medium through which heaven and earth are unified through action, and "action" is only of consequence when it carries *kavannah,* "intention." Prayer is empty without *"kavannah* of the heart." As in social science, following Weber and Schutz, "intention" supplies the difference between "behavior" and "action." What is the proper focus of study for Weber and Schutz is the condition of existence for the Hasid: ". . . it is understandable why Hasidism had no incentive to break loose any stick from the structure of the traditional Law, for according to the Hasidic teaching there could not exist anything that was not to be filled with intention or whose intention could not be discovered" (Buber 1966:127).

Sometimes, however, the intention behind the occurrence is elusive. Yet, in all the conversations and readings in preparation for this study, one theme has presented itself again and again: certainty of the ultimate rationality of the universe, a rationality that may appear to noncomprehending humanity as absurdity. Absurdity is the outcome of an incongruity between faith and experience, and in Jewish thought this conflict between the trust in God's existence and his rational plan for the Jews, and the capriciousness and difficulties of daily existence has produced a literature infused with an appreciation of the Jew's paradoxical situation and a humor that delights in the absurd. A Yiddish proverb says, "If God lived on earth, all his windows would be broken."

If the universe of the Jew is filled with purpose and intention, it is the role of each individual to comprehend and enact that purpose. The Seder is a format that proclaims the purpose of the Jew in history, and through which each person reaffirms the commitment to that purpose —no matter how enigmatic it may sometimes appear. "Israel" means "He who wrestles with God."

The ritual that provides a means of presenting, sorting out, and making experience acceptable and desirable to the people can act as a text for the anthropologist. As a socially constructed and collectively sustained symbolic form, a ritual is an expression of the universe as perceived by the community. Ritual is formalized communication, an exchange of meanings in a particular time and place, and it can be examined as one would examine any artistic expression to gain insight into the culture that generated it. The Seder can permit us to gain a comprehension of what it is to be a "Jew," much as the Oedipus story suggests what it was to be a "man" in Greece. Neither the Greek drama nor the Jewish ritual is a definitive description of all the social forces acting on the society; rather, like all art forms, they are quintessential statements about conditions of existence as seen by the society that creates them. The problem in anthropology is to analyze such artistic social expressions "scientifically," recording actions, words, objects, as accurately as possible through repeated observations, and seeking out the ideas, and the implicit logic of their relationships, which produce the socially shared symbolic system called culture.

No two rituals, although performed according to explicit rules, can be exactly the same to the participants. Symbols are fluid, not fixed; they are polysemic and multivocal, representative and evocative of the social context in which they "exist." No matter how ancient or divine the story that justifies it, a ritual is always an active process that expresses, interprets, and communicates present social experience to the participants. Present experience is the result of the convergence of the traditional teachings, the contingencies of physical survival, the relationships between individuals, and the more existential questions of the reason and purpose of life. As a reflection and projection of the society, the communication of ritual will necessarily include the contradictions and ambiguities of daily life as well as statements of affinity between members.

The contradictions and problems exhibited within the highly affective and generally optimistic context of the Seder are expressive of a system of thought that values dialectic and questioning as a means of discovering the truth. In Jewish life, this has resulted in the patterns of talmudic disputation and in the most extreme splicing of meanings known as *pilpul* ("pepper" or "spice"). Such conscious dichotomizing of meaning and of social experience, which produces the actions discussed in this work, appears to be also expressive of a universal form of thought that underlies the construction of all social forms in all societies.

Culture is fundamentally a symbolic construction on the sensual world; it is the means through which a group of people collectively impose form and hence order on the flux of experience. Culture, then, implies mastery and control. Lévi-Strauss suggests that this mastery and control comes through an implicit and necessary operation of all human thought, a continual process of binary distinction that creates relationships according to the principle of opposition. This relation of opposition is imposed by the mind on all dimensions of experience, by all peoples. The particular "content" of the categories of thought that are constructed as a result of this oppositional relationship will depend on the empirical existence of the society, and so each will have its own "culture," though all are constructed according to the same imperative of thought.

The relation "culture/nature" has been used by Lévi-Strauss to refer to the process through which humans achieve mastery and control over their material world. "Culture" implies "transcendence" over "natural" form, the transformation of the raw into a "cooked" or processed state. All law as well as all technology is "culture," as is ritual, for through such actions of the mind people surpass the givens of their biological selves and their physical environment. The terms "nature" and "culture" provide a means of understanding the imposition of control and order in all domains of experience, whether in the definition of social groups, dietary laws, or the historical and mythological explanation for the society, and are used throughout this study to describe the way in which Jewish thought in particular creates its social universe.

A note is in order about the form of the Hebrew terms being used. With the aim of minimizing confusion in the use of terms unfamiliar to the reader who is not acquainted with Hebrew, I have anglicized words in the plural: matzah becomes "matzahs" and not *matzot*. There is one exception: I have kept "Hasidim" as the plural of Hasid since it is a term of collective identity and more appropriate to the subject matter. Again, because it seems more in keeping with the purpose of understanding the perspective of the culture from within, I have kept the Jewish system of dating. Instead of B.C., I use B.C.E. ("before the common era"); and C.E. ("common era") replaces A.D.

1
"In Each Generation"

"In the East, in the East is my heart,
And I dwell in the end of the West . . ."
Judah HaLevi, Spain,
twelfth century

Seders are observed in every country where Jews reside, among every social class, in one form or another, in even the most difficult circumstances of war, poverty, physical danger. Those who come to the Seder share little except their self-identification as "Jew." Although some participants are extremely pious and learned in the biblical stories and commentaries that provide the rationale for the Seder and a code for daily living, others openly disavow belief in the teachings and exclude themselves from all other ritual participation. Still, these disbelievers come, and the Seder continues to be celebrated. Its persistence provokes one question above all: Why, in an age and civilization in which ritual among Jews is on the decline, is the Seder still vital?

It is through the investigation of the total dynamics and semantics of the ritual, and its relationship to the society's perceived history and experience—its culture—that the answer may be sought.

The commandment to celebrate the festival of Passover is found in the Book of Exodus, where God instructs the Israelites to participate in a sacrificial meal prior to their departure from Egypt, and describes the basic form the commemoration of the event is to take:

> You shall observe the Feast of Unleavened Bread, for on this very day I brought your ranks out of the land of Egypt; you shall observe this day throughout the generations as an institution for all time. In the first month,

1

from the fourteenth day of the month at evening, you shall eat unleavened bread until the twenty-first day of the month at evening. No leaven shall be found in your houses for seven days. For whoever eats what is leavened, that person shall be cut off from the assembly of Israel, whether he is a stranger or a citizen of the country. [12:16-19]

If a stranger who dwells with you would offer the passover to the Lord, all his males must be circumcised; then he shall be admitted to offer it; he shall then be as a citizen of the country. But no uncircumcised person may eat of it. There shall be one law for the citizen and for the stranger who dwells among you. [12:48-49]

The name for the festival, Passover (*Pesah* in Hebrew), is commonly explained as referring to God's "passing over" the houses of the Israelites when he killed the first-born sons of the Egyptians the night before he delivered the Israelites from slavery in Egypt. In the Bible, *Pesah* is applied specifically to the sacrifice that the Israelites ate that night in accordance with God's command. The festival itself is called *Hag HaMatzot,* the Feast of the Unleavened Bread. The term *Hag HaAviv,* the Festival of Spring *(Aviv),* is also used to denote this period.

The Passover ritual as performed today is part of a continual process of ritual evolution begun thousands of years ago, and, in fact, predating the historical event used to justify it. The Bible speaks of the patriarch Abraham's observing the Paschal sacrifice well before the Israelites went to Egypt. The spring festival is apparently the result of the coalescence of the protective paschal celebrations of transient breeders such as Abraham, the agricultural first-fruit festival of the unleavened bread, and the ideas in Exodus. Actions that existed prior to the event in social history became the means through which new ideas crucial to the definition of the community could be expressed.[1]

In the ancient nation of Israel, today's "Festival of Freedom" was celebrated by the gathering of all the Jews at God's Temple in Jerusalem. Each family brought a lamb to be sacrificed in commemoration of the sacrifice eaten the night before the Exodus. In successive groups, as many as would fill the courtyard, they slaughtered the animals, gave

1. There is some argument about the origin of the name for the festival. Some scholars believe the name *Pesah* comes from the root meaning "skipping," and first signified the skipping motions of a lamb and the dancing motions of the participants at the early pastoral sacrifices. This would explain the designation *Pesah* for both the sacrifice and the festival. In this view, the concept "sparing" or "passing over" is a secondary development of the meaning related to the changing historical situation. (*Jewish Encyclopedia* 1909:553). This idea is disputed in the *Encyclopedia Judaica Jerusalem* (1971:173).

some of the blood to the priests to be thrown at the base of the altar, and then roasted the lambs. The meat was eaten with unleavened bread before midnight, following the Biblical command.

Even after the site of the great sacrifices was destroyed, the ritual celebration of Passover continued, but in modified form. In the year 70 C.E. the Temple fell to the Romans. The Jews were banished from Jerusalem and prohibited from teaching the Law or observing their ritual practices on pain of death. It was impossible to continue their life as Jews in Israel, in either a political or religious sense, and so Jews took residence throughout Europe, North Africa, and the Middle East. Although Jews had lived outside of Israel for hundreds of years prior to the fall of the Temple, separation from the land promised them by God had always been voluntary, except for the short period of exile in Babylonia after the fall of the first Temple in 586 B.C.E. Many Jews elected to stay in Babylonia after the restoration of the land to Israel in 515 B.C.E., and Babylonia became a center of scholarship rivaling and even surpassing that of the restored kingdom.

The dispersion after 70 C.E. appeared more complete and the likelihood of return more distant, and it acquired its own descriptive terms: "diaspora," referring to the state of residence abroad, and *galut* ("exile"), the moral counterpart to diaspora, indicating a spiritual as well as a physical distance from God.

The Seder is a creation of and a response to life in the diaspora. One could no longer make a pilgrimage to the Temple; the synagogues of each town were and still are understood as houses of study, prayer, and assembly, but never as replacements for the Temple. Moreover, the people now often lived in small, isolated communities, practicing trades far different from those of their agricultural or pastoral ancestors. As conditions of life were different, so too was the celebration of Passover. A home ceremony replaced one at the Temple, perhaps to avoid the implication that the synagogue had replaced the Temple. The Passover meal had always been celebrated in family groups, and so the move into the home can be seen as a logical modification of the past ceremony. Still, the move appears to reflect changing conceptions of Jewish society. These changes will be explored more fully in later chapters, but suffice it to say here that, in moving the ceremony indoors, the sacrifice was replaced as the main symbol of the ritual by the matzah, and certain practices were added, such as opening the door to welcome the prophet Elijah. The Seder reached the form we know today sometime in the early Middle Ages, but, as indicated above that form continues to be modified in local practice.

The practice of celebrating a Seder on both the first and second nights of the eight-day observance of Passover was developed in the diaspora. In order to be certain that they did not violate ritual observances through calendrical miscalculation, the Jews of the diaspora often repeated the first day of a festival. The first day of Passover was "doubled," as was its ritual, a practice continued today by Orthodox and Conservative Jewish groups. The Reform branch of Judaism has dropped the additional day and Seder, and in Israel also, Passover is celebrated for only seven days.

Two existential problems are present today that rarely troubled the Jew who molded the early Seder: the definition of "Jew" and hence of "community," and disbelief in the historical tale being celebrated at the Seder. Prior to the granting of political rights in western Europe after the French Revolution, and the mass emigration from eastern Europe at the turn of this century, Jewish societies were socially segregated units, defined by internal laws that dictated and clarified boundaries, and by external laws that governed economic and educational mobility. Especially from the time of the Middle Ages on, Jewish residence was confined to particular areas: ghettos in European cities, mellahs in many Arab lands, and the rural "Pale of Settlement" in Poland and the Ukraine. Where social institutions were strong and learning of the sacred-social Law was enforced, "Jewishness" was not an "ethnic definition" or a philosophical system, but rather an identification with a collectivity and a fundamental orientation to the universe that remained unchallenged by alternative systems of knowledge.

Life was not always easy. At various times Jews were excluded from countries, confined to specific trades—often those prohibited to Christians—or forced to obey sumptuary laws or adopt distinctive clothing. Such clothing has had a dual role: while it has emphasized the absolute distinction of the Jews to the outsider, within the community it has reinforced the social identity of the Jew as different, a concept compatible with internal ideology. Such distinctive clothing has been kept by the Orthodox Hasidim as an outward expression of their inner, separated state.

In many places, Jews formed closed, corporate communities, *kehillot,* which had the power to negotiate social rights. Membership in the wider society was defined through Christian or Moslem association, overtly before the rise of "secular" nations, more subtly thereafter.

Weber has termed the Jews a "pariah people," a hereditary social group lacking political autonomy, carrying social disprivilege, with distinctive economic functions and a complex of religious beliefs and obligations that preclude their integration into the society about them (1964:108–9). In this position, the Jews were often the object of the forces of social unrest that exploded in the massacres of the Crusades, the peasant uprisings of seventeenth-century eastern Europe, and the pogroms of nineteenth- and twentieth-century Russia. Even in those times and places where fortunes were better, as in Spain under the Moors, the individual's primary identity and his relationship to others was dependent upon his membership in the community of Jews. As much as he might chafe at the restrictions and beliefs of his society, his definition as a Jew by the outside society, and the limitations it placed on him concerning his economic and physical survival, worked to keep him "at home." Outright conversion or intermarriage meant severing ties to family and friends to enter an unknown world: if he took either action, the family said the prayer for the dead.

With the coming of political emancipation, and with the emigration of many Jews to America, ritual observance has declined, and with it the clarity of the perception of the boundaries of the community. Douglas sees ritual forms hardening in times of social stress as the community uses its individual and collective bodies to express the tension and anxieties it perceives socially (1970:32). Through a strict and unwavering adherence to form one may influence fate; ritual becomes a way of participating in the divine plan. Conversely, in a freer social atmosphere, ritual forms are relaxed. Whatever the reasons, and there are many, few Jews in America today are very learned in the Law or adhere to the strict ritual code that developed during the Middle Ages in the closed communities of Europe, Asia, and North Africa. Yet, as Sklare (1967), Gans (1958), Kramer and Leventman (1961), and others have pointed out, they remain cognizant of their "Jewishness." Arendt (1968) considers this "Jewishness" less a social statement than a psychological condition, but, even so, it still presumes an awareness or allegiance outside the self, a participation in some sort of extended, though ill-defined, community.

Jewish society has always had its doubters, its *apikoros*, but what was in the past an isolated phenomenon has become today a part of reality for the secularized Jew. For some people today, the factuality of the story is important if they are to participate in the world view emanating from it. These celebrants seek to substantiate the Exodus story with archeological findings and historical records. Others treat the story as primitive myth and discount it. But either perspective begs the question of the importance or relevance of the accuracy of the historical record for the work of the Seder. It may be that the event did indeed take place around 1270 B.C.E. (Klein 1973:3), but, as will be shown later, "history's" role in the Seder is not descriptive but creative and definitive: "history" locates the celebrants in a temporal dimension according to a divine plan. The past is described as a period of utter darkness that is forever banished by the community's relationship with God; the future is not a series of dates but a period of fulfillment; and the present, no matter how good or bad the experience of the individual community, is a state of movement forward. History is the framework that defines the Jew of the present—no matter where or when he celebrates the Seder—by his existence in this in-between state, and it is this eternal, conclusively inconclusive identity that is displayed and played with through the symbolic actions of the Seder evening.

2
The Ritual

Order is the basic requirement
for communication.
     Mary Douglas
     Natural Symbols

The name of the ritual, Seder, or "Order," carries meanings
in Jewish life that unite the events of the evening with ideas met
throughout the year. In Jewish thought, "order" is inextricably part of
the concept of social action.

In any society, to order experience is to create a universe. A meaningful world emerges as form and distinction are imposed upon the
natural world and upon sensation; the definition given to one term
simultaneously creates and defines its opposite, as "nature" defines
"culture." The principles that guide the distinctions made in constructing this social reality vary with the society, but they are justified by an
appeal to a higher, immutable reality, whether called "self-evident"
truths, categorical imperatives, or God. In Judaism, the rationality of
God is assumed, and it provides the model for the conduct of one's life.

In Jewish thought, order is not explained as a binary process but as
the way through which man may know God and so participate in God's
work on earth. God's logic may be hidden, much as the principles of the
physical ordering of the universe may be elusive, but that does not
mean it does not exist. As scientists today look to the galaxy, called
"order" in Hebrew, for answers to the operations of the universe, Jews
look through the divinely given Torah. The first book of the Talmud,
the Mishnah, is divided into six sections, or "orders," and the daily
prayer book that guides man's approach to God is called the Siddur,

7

from the root word for "order." Through its name, the Seder ritual focuses attention on an intrinsic attribute of God and on the highest mode of action for man.

The Seder, therefore, acts on two levels as a means of communication: as a medium of relationship between man and God, and as a structure that governs the relationships between the participants in the evening's events. The ritual exhibits Douglas's premise that each system of communication must contain its own internal principles of clarity and coherence (1973). What first appears as redundancy or as a superfluous game is actually part of a system of meaning created to ensure the goals of the ritual: to produce a vision of both history and eternity compatible with the experiences of the celebrants, and, above all, to provide the community with a picture of itself that will sustain it throughout the coming year. How the Seder involves each person as author and audience in the creation and conveyance of this "idealized experience" is described in the following pages.

The order of the Seder is set out in the Haggadah, or "telling," a book of stories, biblical passages, songs, hymns of praise, benedictions, and instructions for the use of the ceremonial items. The Haggadah was developed during the years following the destruction of the Temple, building on and adapting features of the Temple practice to new circumstances. The oldest passage is thought to be that which calls the matzah "the bread of affliction," probably dating from the sixth century B.C.E. in Babylonia; the Psalms and the Four Questions were also part of the Temple ceremony.

The Haggadah has been printed in the most elaborate and humble forms, in Hebrew and in the vernaculars, in over thirty-five hundred editions. Today, many Haggadahs are edited to accommodate the diversity of knowledge and experience of the participants. These Haggadahs often include references to contemporary events in the form of additional readings or actions, and occasionally traditional passages are restated to make them more "relevant." Yet despite these improvisations, virtually all versions of the Haggadah include the traditional readings and sequence that are the core of the Seder service, and therefore the passages quoted on the following pages are common to the very many Haggadahs read in the preparation of this book. Since it is assumed in this study that the Seder and its Haggadah are part of a continually evolving process of social creation, no one Haggadah has been considered definitive. However, the Haggadah edited by Cecil

Roth (1959) has been particularly useful as a reference since Roth provides more detailed instructions and historical and social commentary than are usually offered. The quotations from the Haggadah in this chapter are from *Let My People Go: A Haggadah,* edited by Mark Podwal. This Haggadah, used for its clarity of language, depicts the "Egyptian" oppressors in Nazi and Soviet uniforms.

The Haggadah's many editions are often art forms, freely embellished with color, stylized printing, and humorous pictorial commentary on current practices, such as parents portrayed in European peasant dress and children in modern clothing, smoking cigarettes. The art work often reflects the artistic style of the land of residence. In a culture that bans iconography in its holy books and buildings, the Haggadah has been a permissible outlet for artistic expression and appreciation. However, today the most common Haggadahs are those printed inexpensively so that each person at a Seder may have a copy and thus participate more easily.

The designs and exact content may vary with the many Haggadahs, but the basic order of the symbolic actions rarely does. Consequently, despite local idiosyncracies, a man from third-century Egypt or eighteenth-century Poland would recognize the ritual as a Seder—different from his, but somehow the same.

It is the order of the Haggadah and the redundancy in ritual that permit such discrepancies. The words of the Haggadah and the taste of the matzah join with other actions and sensations of the ritual to carry society's messages on many levels, so that the ideas that necessitate the convocation can be received. If there is "noise" in one channel—if the individual is not attuned to the allusions in one form of communication—he will be reached in another way. The symbols refer to and support each other. The learned Orthodox Jew, who reads the Torah all the way through each year and studies the Talmud, will draw on a wealth of associations denied the secularized Jew. Although these rich, multivocal allusions will be lost to the less formally educated Jew, their place may be taken by referents from contemporary life that somehow seem to "fit" the mood of the Seder. In practice, the Seders may contain differences, but both will fulfill their function of teaching and reinforcing society's values, and of making these values consistent with the perceived world.

The Seder is quite consciously convened as a teaching event whose performance is incumbent on each person:

> And thou shall tell thy son in that day, saying, "It is because of what the Lord did for me when I went from Egypt." [Exodus 13:8]

The Haggadah explicitly connects the present community with past deliverance:

> In every generation, every Jew must regard himself as though he, personally, were brought out of Egypt, as it is said: "And you shall tell your son on that day, saying: It is because of what the Lord did for *me* when I left Egypt." It was not our ancestors alone that the Holy One, blessed be He, redeemed from Egypt, but He redeemed us with them . . .

The Haggadah points out and explains the symbols. These explanations are themselves part of the meaning structure of the symbol, being the explicit part of a complex of implicit ideas that cling to the item either because of its use in other rituals throughout the year, or because of ideas met in daily worship or daily life. In recognizing and commenting on this difference between the literal explanation and the more latent ones, mystical Judaism has provided yet another set of meanings for Jewish life and for the Seder.

All these "orderings," "meanings," and "constructions of reality" must be taken out of the realm of ideas and wedded to each member of society if they are to have any practical function in guiding his or her daily actions. The structure of the Seder permits, indeed requires, each person to join the ritual whatever his or her degree of learning, belief, social status, or ritual participation at other times. "Society" is defined in its widest sense, as opposed to many other ritual procedures in Jewish culture that exclude people because of their age or sex. All communication that takes place at the Seder must be available to everyone.

Formal public ritual is like a game that everyone agrees to play. The participants consent to abide by the rules of the evening and to let the decisions concerning their own actions be taken out of their hands and placed in the Haggadah's program. For the success of the game, they allow themselves to be freed for the evening from the mentally divisive process of decision making, which focuses the mind on ideas in opposition, and also tacitly agree to ignore the personal matters and status considerations that separate individuals in nonritual time. In relaxing the barriers that divide people mentally and socially, the focus of the evening may now be socially shared ideological considerations and not private concerns.

The structure speaks of "constancy" and inclusion despite the discrepancies between the ideals of social harmony and the daily dishar-

monies between people and between ideological promise and its realization. Such internal differences are not forgotten at the Seder; they
may even surface at times; but their effect is softened as the order of
the Haggadah, and not any individual's will, assumes control.

The particular complex of meanings that evolves through the action of the ritual may be unique to the Seder, but the items and actions
that carry the messages are hardly special to Jewish society. The foods
employed are common to everyday life and ritual throughout the
world. Salt, yeast, greens, eggs, water, and unleavened bread are everyday items in North Africa and the Middle East, and unleavened bread
and wine are the core of the Catholic Mass. The form of the Seder—
ritual actions preceding and following a communal meal—is one of the
most common forms of social assembly, and the Seder recognizes this
affinity in explaining the direction to recline at certain points "as in the
custom of free men at a Roman feast." The paschal sacrifice that has
been supplanted by the Seder was a feature of Middle Eastern desert
life, and the Passover is still celebrated today with such a sacrifice by
the Samaritans who live on the West Bank of the Jordan. Yet, when the
Seder raises its central symbol, the matzah, it is raising a set of ideas
specific to Jewish culture. Despite its similar form, matzah is not the
unleavened bread of the nomad or the communicant; it is a particular
social construction concentrating and conveying some of the most important concepts in Jewish culture.

The Seder of the Jews of central and eastern Europe, the Ashkenazic Jews, will be discussed as an ideal form, since this is the model
that most influences practices in America today. Any particular Seder
will, of course, contain its own improvised variations as the celebrants
create a living, expressive medium from the ideal model.

Although "Ashkenaz" specifically refers in Hebrew to Germany,
the term has come to include all Jews from central and eastern Europe
and their descendants. There was a migration of Jews eastward to Poland and Russia from Germany in the latter part of the Middle Ages, and
this accounts for the German-Hebrew or Yiddish dialect of the Russian
Jews. The descendants of the Jews who left Spain (*Sepharad* in Hebrew)
after the expulsion in 1492 are called "Sephardic." Most settled in the
Mediterranean countries of Europe and North Africa, Turkey, and
Syria; some went to Holland, England, and America. A third term,
"Oriental," refers to the Jews of the Middle East, India, and Asia and
the non-Sephardic Jews of North Africa. (Sometimes the terms "Sephardic" and "Oriental" are used interchangeably to refer to all non-

Ashkenazic Jews.) Each settlement has exerted a different influence on the local Jewish culture, which, in turn, affects the performance and meanings of the Seder. Today, despite a high degree of uniformity among the Haggadahs, these different populations have different ways of handling the materials of the Seder, which appear to reflect slightly different world views. Although common Sephardic or Oriental modifications of the Ashkenazic model are discussed here, they are included merely to highlight the Ashkenazic practice, and not as a statement of Sephardic or Oriental culture. Ritual must be looked at as a mesh whose meanings interact, not as a collection of distinct items with their own history and rationale. Sephardic and Oriental variants seem to point to a vision of the world that is less harsh than the Ashkenazic, but this is only an impression, a suspicion, and not a conclusion valid in the absence of an analysis that systematically includes all the actions and explanations given at the Sephardic and Oriental Seders, and an exploration of the social setting and political fortunes of these communities.

The Haggadah's instructions are for the Seder evening only, but they are part of a much wider body of rules and regulations contained in the Torah, Talmud, and custom that determine the actions of the individual and the community in the weeks preceding Passover. The Seder comes as a climax or summation of all the actions of these weeks, and as such, it is the ultimate realization of a particular state of being both for the house and for the person. To achieve this perfect state, the rules dictate one's behavior and turn one's thoughts to Passover long before the fourteenth day of the Hebrew month of Nisan.

Because the words of the yearly liturgy exhort compliance with God's laws "because I am the Lord thy God who brought you out of the land of Egypt," the Jew's mind is kept focused throughout the year on the ideas to be presented more dramatically at the Seder. On the Sabbath immediately before Passover, the Great Sabbath, the focus sharpens. A portion of the Haggadah is read in the synagogue, as is a passage from the Bible in which the prophet Malachi foretells the coming of the prophet Elijah. Elijah will prepare the way for the Messiah by bringing peace within each family:

> And he shall turn the heart of the fathers to the children, and the heart of the children to their fathers . . . [Malachi 3:24]

If the mental preparation is year-long, the actual physical preparations begin about a month before the festival with an exhaustive house-cleaning. The specific aim of the cleaning is to remove all leaven, or *hometz*. *Hometz* is defined as any grain that ferments on decomposition, namely, wheat, barley, spelt, oats, and rye.[1] Other fermentation is permitted. All foods that contain *hometz* and all foods that have been exposed to *hometz* must be removed from the house and replaced with new items produced in complete segregation from *hometz*. The wheat and potato flour used for the festival are produced under carefully controlled conditions to ensure that no fermentation takes place.

Hometz that a family or business such as a bakery does not want to destroy may be locked away and "sold" for the duration of the festival to a non-Jew. Contracts are drawn up; a small transfer of money takes place; and the *hometz* is legally gone. A community might appoint an agent to arrange for the "selling" of all its *hometz,* and after the holiday, the exchange is reversed.

All cooking utensils and implements are ritually cleaned or exchanged for special holiday ones. Ovens are heated until they glow, and pots are scoured and washed in boiling water. All utensils used for baking, and earthenware, which might have absorbed leavened products, must be put away. Counters are covered, and the Passover dishes brought out.

On the evening before Passover, there is a ritual search for leaven, *Bedikas Hometz.* Although by this time the house has been thoroughly cleaned and the leaven for the morning's breakfast carefully set aside, this "search" formally announces that all the home conditions for Passover have been met. A known quantity of leaven, usually ten pieces of bread, is placed on window sills and in other locations in the home to be found by the father as he searches with a single candle, feather, and wooden spoon. The leaven, feather, and spoon are wrapped in a cloth or newspaper, taken outside the house overnight, and burned in the early morning hours, with a final declaration that the house is emptied of leaven: "All leaven that is in my possession, which has escaped my notice and which I have not removed, is hereby regarded as nonexistent or as mere dust of the earth." Any leaven left from breakfast will be burned. Matzah cannot be eaten until the Seder.

The "search" is actually a drama by and for the actors in which they are ideal men bringing an ideal purity to the home by conforming to

1. Rice and millet rot and do not ferment, and so technically are permitted. In Ashkenazic communities it was felt that allowing these grains might introduce confusion, and so they have been prohibited along with "doubtful pulse" of beans, peas, maize, and peanuts. In general, Ashkenazic interpretations of the Law have been more stringent than the Sephardic. In Sephardic communities, rice is commonly eaten on Passover.

God's command, "No leaven shall be found in your houses for seven days." Played by candlelight, structured like a child's game of hide-and-seek, the Search for the Leaven turns the mind of even the youngest child to the coming days.

Early in the morning, before Passover begins, the first-born sons attend a ceremony at the synagogue known as the Fast of the First-born. This fast is commonly explained as a commemoration of God's protection of the Israelite first-born sons the night before the Exodus. The fast is circumvented if a first-born son is celebrating a joyous event. Since the completion of the study of a tractate of the Talmud is considered just such a joyous event, one of the first-born arranges to have the reading end coincident with the eve of Passover (the morning before). Instead of a fast, the first-born share cake and wine. In the morning also, the "selling" of the *hometz* takes place.

In the late afternoon, while the most pious men go to the ritual bath, the table is set with the family's finest linens and dishes. The cloth is white, the platters and wine glasses perfect, there are candles and flowers on the table, and a Haggadah is at each place. All is ready so that the Seder may start when the men return from the synagogue.

The table is also set with the items that are to be used to illustrate the narration. Sweet red wine is placed near the leader's seat, and a plate of hard-boiled eggs and a dish of salt water—said to represent the tears of the slaves—are nearby. In the center of the table is a wine goblet to be filled at the proper time for the prophet Elijah. Before the leader is the "Seder plate," which holds the other symbolic foods used this evening:

a roasted shankbone (*zero'a,* "forearm") is described in the Haggadah as the representative of the Paschal sacrifice. A piece of meat must be attached to the bone. "Forearm" is explained as referring to the outstretched arm of God when he delivered the Israelites from Egypt.

a roasted or baked egg (*hagigah,* "sacrifice") is said to commemorate the additional sacrifices at the Temple as well as the destruction of the Temple. Kasher says the egg was chosen as a symbol of the sacrifice because in Aramaic the word for egg is *be-tzah,* which is derived from the phrase "Come, Eternal, and redeem us" (1950:13).

bitter herbs *(maror)* are said to recall the bitterness of slavery in Egypt. Horseradish or the core of romaine lettuce is used.

haroset ("clay"), fruits, nuts, spices, and fermented liquid, blended into a paste and popularly interpreted as a reminder of the mortar the Israelites used while working as slaves in Egypt. The most common ingredients of the *haroset* are apples, raisins, walnuts or almonds, cinnamon, and sweet wine, but there is much variation in this list depending on locale.

greens *(karpas),* celery, lettuce, parsley, etc., representing spring, are sometimes associated with the hyssop that was dipped in the blood of the Paschal lamb to mark the doorways of the Israelites before the Exodus. Raw onions or potatoes may be substituted for the celery or parsley; both vegetables produce green shoots.

The most common arrangement of the symbolic foods on the Seder plate in Europe and America today is pictured in figure 1. This is the arrangement suggested by the kabbalist Rabbi Isaac Luria in Safed, Israel, in the sixteenth century and presented in the Code of Jewish Law (vol. 3, 118:8). There are two frequent modifications of this arrangement: sometimes the lower portion of bitter herbs is eliminated, and very often the matzahs are on another plate for convenience. The three matzahs are placed under a cloth, separated by the folds of a napkin.

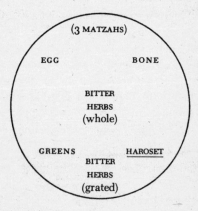

Figure 1.
Arrangement of symbols according to Rabbi Isaac Luria and the Code of Jewish Law.

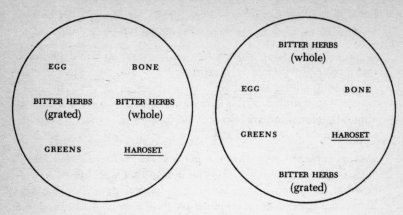

Figure 2.
Modern modifications of the traditional arrangement.

The Seder plate has become an art form, made in pottery, china, lucite, or metal, and embellished with color and design. The artistic requirements of the plate may have generated the two very common variations of the traditional arrangement found in modern homes and pictured in figure 2. In both cases, the egg, bone, greens, and *haroset* are in the same position, but the bitter herbs are placed either at the upper and lower center or at center right and center left, so that the symbols form a circle.[2]

The plate is set before the leader's chair, which faces the main door of the house if possible. On his chair is a cushion so that he may recline throughout the meal, and nearby is a white robe, or *kittel,* which he will put on at the proper time.[3] After the housewife lights the festival candles, the family and friends take their seats around the table. The wife customarily sits at her husband's right, but otherwise there is no prescribed seating arrangement.

The evening is divided into three main sections. The first and last deal with the past and the future history and hopes of the community,

2. It has been German custom to use a three-tiered metal Seder plate. The foods are placed on the top, and the matzahs are placed below on three shelves, which are often closed by doors.

3. As "free men," all may recline during the ceremony, but there are certain times when each person must recline. The Code of Jewish Law exempts women from reclining, but in popular practice women participate as fully as they are able. The *kittel* is worn in the eastern European tradition, but not at other Seders, and is sometimes omitted. Because of the redundancy of information in the ritual, its omission will not seriously affect the total exchange of messages.

and are separated by a feast. The first and last sections are in turn divided into action complexes with specific names that mark the progression through the order of the ritual. While substitutions and improvisations may occur in the Seder, it is in the manner of enacting this order, and not in the order itself, that change almost always takes place.

The Seder proceeds as follows. First, the wine cups are filled.

KADDESH (Sanctification)

The following benediction is said over the wine by the leader:

> Blessed art Thou, O Lord our God, King of the Universe, Creator of the fruit of the vine. Blessed art Thou, O Lord our God, King of the Universe, for having exalted us above all nations, and for having sanctified us with Thy commandments. In love, hast Thou, O Lord our God, given us solemn days of joy and festive seasons of gladness, even this Feast of Unleavened Bread, the season of our liberation, a holy convocation to commemorate the departure from Egypt. Thou hast chosen us and sanctified us above all peoples, and Thou hast made us share the holy festivals, to be observed in happiness and gladness. Blessed art Thou, O Lord, who has sanctified Israel and the festive seasons.

> Blessed art Thou, O Lord our God, King of the universe, who hast kept us alive and hast sustained us to reach this festive season.

The wine is drunk by all, reclining to the left. The leader puts on the *kittel*.

U'RHATZ (Wash hands)

The children bring a pitcher, bowl, and towel to the leader, who pours water over his hands without reciting a benediction. At many Seders, everyone, and not just the leader, washes his or her hands at this time.

KARPAS (Greens)

The leader distributes some of the greens to each person, who dips them in salt water and eats them after the following blessing (the customary blessing over produce):

> Blessed art Thou, O Lord our God, King of the Universe, Creator of the fruit of the earth.

YAHATZ (Dividing)

The leader divides the middle matzah of the three into two unequal parts. He wraps the larger portion in a napkin, hides it in the cushions of his chair, and replaces the smaller piece. The piece that is taken from the table is the *afikoman,* "dessert." As the last food to be eaten in the ritual, it is necessary for the completion of the Seder. At some point during the recitation of the Haggadah, the children will "steal" the *afikoman,* or the leader will hide it for the children to find. When the Seder calls for the *afikoman,* the children will refuse to return it to the leader until he pays a ransom, usually a small gift.

MAGEED (Narration)

If the ceremonial plate is separate from the one holding the matzahs, it is removed from the table at this point. If they are the same, only the egg and bone are removed. The matzahs are then uncovered by the leader, who raises and displays them to the company. Those nearest the leader put out their hands to assist in supporting the tray; the leader recites the *HaLachma Anya:*

> Lo! this is the bread of affliction which our fathers ate in the land of Egypt. Let all who are hungry come and eat. Let all who are in want come and celebrate the Passover with us. This year we are here, next year we shall be in the land of Israel. This year we are in servitude, next year we shall be free men.

The matzahs are put down and covered; the ceremonial plate is returned, or the egg and bone replaced; and the second cup of wine is filled. Then the youngest child, male or female, rises and asks the Four Questions:

> Why is this night different from all other nights?
>
> On all other nights, we may eat either leavened or unleavened bread; on this night, we eat only unleavened bread.
>
> On all other nights, we eat all kinds of herbs; on this night we eat only bitter herbs.
>
> On all other nights, we do not dip (the vegetables) even once; on this night, we have to dip them twice.
>
> On all other nights, we eat either in a sitting or in a reclining position; on this night, we all recline.[4]

The matzahs are uncovered. The answer begins with:

> We were Pharaoh's slaves in Egypt. But the Lord our God brought us out of there with a mighty hand and an outstretched arm. Had not the Holy One, blessed be He, brought forth our fathers from Egypt, we, our chil-

---

4. After the fall of the Temple, this question replaced one asking why, on this night, the Paschal sacrifice must be roasted.

dren, and our children's children would have remained Pharaoh's slaves in Egypt. Therefore, even if all of us were wise, men of understanding, sages, and well versed in the Torah, it would still be our duty to tell the story of deliverance from Egypt. And the more one tells of the deliverance from Egypt, the more praiseworthy he is.

The narrative explains why the sages decided that the ritual should be held at night, and then the story of the Four Sons is told: the wise, the wicked, the naive, the one who does not know how to ask questions about the ritual. The narration continues with the story of the Exodus. The matzahs are covered, the full goblet is raised, and all recite:

And this promise has been our fathers' support and ours; for not one tyrant has risen up against us to destroy us, but in every generation tyrants have sought to destroy us, and the Holy One, blessed be He, has delivered us from their hands.

The goblet is set down, the matzahs are uncovered, and the narration continues. The Ten Plagues are recounted. A drop of wine is spilled from the cup at the mention of each plague. Sometimes the little finger is dipped into the wine each time a plague is recited, and a bit of wine is sprinkled on the plate below. Mnemonic words are said: The initial letters of each plague are formed into three words and a drop of wine is spilled at the recitation of each word. After more narration, the hymn of thanksgiving *Dayaynoo* ("It Would Have Sufficed for Us") is sung loudly and quickly. The leader shows and explains the three ancient symbols of Passover, the bone, the matzah, and the herbs. The symbols are introduced with the passage:

Rabban Gamaliel said: "Whoever does not mention the meaning of these three symbols, the Paschal lamb, the unleavened bread, and the bitter herbs, has not fulfilled his obligation."

The bone may not be raised during the explanation, but the matzah and the bitter herbs may be either pointed out or raised. After the symbols are explained, all say:

In every generation, every Jew must regard himself as though he, personally, were brought out of Egypt . . .

The matzahs are covered, and the goblet raised. *Hallel,* hymns of praise, are recited, and a benediction is said over the second cup of wine, which is drunk reclining to the left. The matzahs are uncovered.

RAHTZAH (Washing)

Each person pours water over his hands and says the ritual benediction.

MOTZEE (Benediction over Bread)

The leader takes the matzahs and says the usual benediction over bread:

Blessed be the Lord our God, King of the universe, who brings forth bread from the earth.

MATZAH (Benediction over the Unleavened Bread)

He then puts the lower matzah down and says the benediction specific to Passover:[5]

Blessed be the Lord our God, King of the universe, who sanctified us with His commandments, and has commanded us to eat unleavened bread.

MAROR (Bitter Herbs)

The leader distributes a piece of the bitter herb dipped in *haroset*. The *haroset* is shaken off and the following benediction is said before eating:

Blessed be the Lord our God, King of the Universe, who sanctified us with His commandments, and has commanded us to observe eating bitter herbs.

The participant must not recline while eating the bitter herbs dipped in *haroset*.

KOREKH (Combining)

The leader breaks the undermost matzah into pieces, makes sandwiches of grated herbs and matzah, and distributes them.[6] This is called the "Hillel sandwich," in honor of the first-century scholar who is said to have originated it. The sandwich is eaten while reclining to the left, after saying:

Thus was Hillel accustomed to do at the time the Temple still stood: He combined unleavened bread and bitter herbs and ate them together, in order to comply with the instruction: "With unleavened bread and bitter herbs, they shall eat the Passover sacrifice."

The Seder plate is removed.

5. Some raise only the upper two for both benedictions.
6. Some people again dip the whole herb briefly in *haroset,* or, if grated herbs are used, place a bit of *haroset* in the sandwich.

SHULHAN ARUKH (The Set or Prepared Table)

The meal is served, preceded by dipping the hard-boiled eggs in salt water and eating them. The only directive concerning the meal is that no meat roasted over fire may be served, since such meat would make the meal appear an enactment and not a commemoration of the Passover sacrifice. The foods served are generally traditional items, and they vary greatly with the locale. All efforts are made to make the food abundant and the meal as festive as possible. Additional wine is permitted during the meal.

TZAFUN *(Afikoman)*

The leader "finds" that the *afikoman,* or "dessert," is missing and bargains for its return in order to continue the Seder. As the representative of the sacrifice, the *afikoman* is the last food of the Passover ritual, and it must be eaten before midnight, as the original sacrifice was eaten before midnight in Exodus. The *afikoman* is broken and a piece given to each person at the table. It is eaten reclining to the left.

BAREKH (Grace after Meals)

The wine cups are filled. The grace now said is the usual grace recited after meals. The cup of wine, obligatory at the Seder, is optional at other times. A benediction is said over the wine, and the wine is drunk, reclining to the left. Elijah's cup is now filled,[7] the door is opened by anyone present, and all rise and say:

> O pour out Thy wrath upon the nations that know Thee not, and upon the kingdoms that call not upon Thy name. For they have devoured Jacob, and laid waste his land. Pour out Thy indignation upon them, and let the fierceness of Thy anger overtake them. Pursue them in anger, and destroy them from under the heavens of the Lord.

The door is closed and all are seated. The fourth cup of wine is filled, and a long *Hallel* is read, which mixes hopes of redemption with praise to God. The fourth and last cup of wine is drunk, reclining to the left. Another passage is read asking for the rebuilding of Jerusalem, and then come the closing lines.

7. Roth instructs that the cup for Elijah be placed on the table and filled after the door is opened (1959:52).

NIRTZAH (Accepted)

The Seder of the Passover is now complete, according to the laws, rules
and customs. As we have been privileged to celebrate it this year, may we
be worthy to actually offer it in the Holy Land. O Pure One, who abides
in the Temple, raise up Thy numberless people. O speedily lead the
branches Thou has planted, as free men to Zion, with songs of rejoicing.
Next year in Jerusalem!

After the conclusion of the narrative, about midnight, it is customary to sing a few additional hymns praising God's benevolence and
urging redemption, as well as the Song of Songs of Solomon. Some are
based on chapters from the Torah ("And It Came to Pass at Midnight");
others are allegories (*Chad Gadya,* "One Only Kid")[8] or composed of
simple, repetitive words set to European folk tunes. The evening ends
with the spirited singing of these songs.

8. This song, which describes the empires that have swallowed the Jewish people,
only to be in turn swallowed by God, is often compared to the English rhyme "This Is
the House that Jack Built." It is set to a French or German folk tune of the fourteenth
century or earlier.

3

An Ordered Universe

In our tradition, danger is called mixture, the enemy is called chaos. To be Jewish is to live separate from others but not against others. His whole life the Jew is committed to separating light from darkness, Sabbath from the rest of the week, the pure from the impure, and sacred from the profane, the return from the exile, life from death. . . . To mingle categories is to destroy them.

Elie Wiesel
The Oath

Jewish culture, concerned as it is with creating order through distinction, is also concerned with concepts that either uphold or threaten these distinctions. Where order is perceived as divine, disorder is not only a threat to the society's comprehension of its universe, but a profanation as well. The more the society clarifies its distinctions, the more it simultaneously prohibits anything that would weaken them. Yet people must continually deal with the gray, ambiguous areas not totally encompassed by strict definitions: "twilight" can appear to "exist" as well as dark and light, and the diaspora itself is conceived of as an indeterminate state.

In its account of the wanderings of the freed slaves in the desert of Sinai, the Torah treats the problems of such unclearly defined states. The apparent dangers these threats to order suggest and the mechanisms used for conversion from one defined state to another are problems that are part of Jewish thought long after the Seder is completed. In order to understand the importance of the story of the Exodus for Jewish experience throughout the year, it is necessary to see first how the Torah deals with distinction and then how it presents the idea of transition.

23

The story of the Exodus contains within it a rationale for the existence of the Jews as an eternally distinct people, and also provides a metaphor for the Jews' existence as a socially marginal community. As a form that explains how the society came into being, Exodus serves as the "creation myth" of the Jews as a people, as opposed to the myth of the creation of the earth found in Genesis. Like Genesis, Exodus deals with matters of separation and distinction, but Exodus is also a story of passages, of transitional states between fixed points, between absolute slavery in Egypt and absolute freedom in the Promised Land. In its description of how the Israelite slaves were brought by God out of Egypt, received the Torah, and reaffirmed their covenant with God at Mount Sinai, Exodus is the story that once and for all times has given the Jews their self-definition as a people whose existence and purposes are inextricably conditioned to the will of God.

The creation story in Genesis concerns the creation of the physical universe and of the human being; it also describes Abraham's discovery of God. But God's relationship to Abraham is an individual one. Abraham is circumcised, but the relationship is not otherwise marked or committed to an external code. Until Sinai, individuals, the patriarchs and Moses, are the media of relationship between God and man. In Exodus, the Law is given to the people as a whole, and the Law becomes coterminous with society. The individual is forever subordinated to the community as regulated by the Torah. It is the Law that creates the society, and the ex-slaves who leave Egypt, argue with Moses, and construct a golden calf as another, more tangible god, are changed by it into a purposeful social unit.

Like creation myths in other cultures, Exodus tells of the intrusion of the sacred into the world of man and of the relationship of the community with its god. Creation myths are usually recounted in times rich in ritual. The only ritual in Jewish life specifically connected with Genesis is the observance of the Sabbath, when each person is to imitate God's rest from labor; however, the creation story itself is not singled out for discussion. The story of Exodus, in contrast, is retold or alluded to in the daily and the Sabbath liturgy and on every major festival, and the highly ritualistic days of Passover are devoted to its celebration. Hannukah and Purim commemorate Jewish victories also, over the Syrians and over the Persian despot Haman (today understood as a Hitler prototype), but these are considered minor holidays, and their ritual observance is much less elaborate.

The God of both the physical and social creation myths acts according to principles of order. He separates, makes distinctions, categorizes, and so creates. In Genesis, creation is the imposition of order on chaotic nature and the strict definition of categories. God distinguishes light from dark, heavenly bodies from earthly ones, sea, land, and air creatures, man from God, woman from man, rest days from work days. In Exodus, God also creates through separation. The people, separated from Egypt, are to be as clearly distinguished as light from dark, and such separation is just as divinely ordained. Each Saturday evening, as the Sabbath light wanes and the dark of the work week begins, the observant Jew says the *Havdalah* ("distinction") prayer:

> Blessed art Thou, O Lord our God, King of the universe, who makest a distinction between holy and profane, between light and darkness, between Israel and the heathen nations, between the seventh day and the six working days. Blessed art Thou, O Lord, who makest a distinction between holy and profane.

Not only does Exodus clarify the distinction between Jews and other peoples, but it also displays through the concept of creation the basic distinction between God and man. God's creative power is expressed as absolute, as an intrusion of divine power into the universe that separates, once and for all time, the light from the dark, the Jew from the gentile. The power to separate finally is also the power to change matter from one state to another: the Israelites become God's eternal people at Sinai. God's power of absolute conversion is invoked each time the society wishes to proclaim a different status for a social item, each time a profaned object is purified, a child "becomes" a man, or a gentile "becomes" a Jew.

In contrast with God's power to create with finality, the state of being human is the state of continual creation. God may create the eternal distinction of Jew and gentile with one act of revelation—one intrusion into the material world—but the Jews can only realize their unique state through repeated, minute discriminations made according to the Law. The word *kadosh*, "holy," comes from the root meaning "separateness" and indicates discrimination in an action in order to make it conform with the Law. Holiness is unity, as found in the indivisibility of God, a state of total agreement with God, a state of completion and fulfillment. The *Kedusha* prayer in congregational worship announces, "Holy, holy, holy is the Lord of hosts; the whole world is full of his glory." The holy, as that which embodies the Law and hence God, pervades daily life; it is in the proper way to treat a neighbor, prepare a food, or incorporate a new member into the society. By keeping an awareness of God and the Law in routine, daily actions, each person is constantly reminded that his own existence is part of a system of order that governs all phenomena. The profane lacks God's inspiration; it is disorder, confusion, incompletion. The Law may be fixed, but experience is not; the never ending process of discrimination that separates holy from profane and brings the society closer to the standard set by God makes daily life a process of becoming, a perpetual transition. God's creation in Exodus therefore sets the condition for the life of each person.

The process of continually creating their own society demands that the Jews pay very strict attention to the principles of order and classification, and to maintaining the integrity of categorical boundaries. Separation is the principle that explains the construction of the universe and society. In the most ordinary of activities, the Jew pays attention to principles of discrimination, not for their own sake, but because such minute discrimination is understood as man's way of enacting the discrimination inherent in the universe—in Jewish interpretation, the manner in which God acts. Each time the Jew looks to the heavenly bodies, it is "Order" he sees.

Order also appears to give man power and control over the flux and potential chaos of the world of experience. In everyday life, categorical distinction and definition through the relation of opposites have become the common mode of thought and action. The definitional categories the Jew imposes on his material and ideational world are, as in structuralist theory, "empty forms" applicable to the perception of any phenomenon of social life, be it food, sexual roles, or social groups. The process of filling these "empty forms" through classification according to any perceived similarity simultaneously fills the opposing category. If only certain animals may be domesticated and eaten, because of split hooves or for any other reason, then others immediately become "wild" and inedible.

This "structuralist" concern with opposition and the principles of discrimination and classification reaches its apogee in talmudic disputation. The "received" Torah must be endlessly clarified to understand God's thoughts and purposes and so make the Law operable in everyday life. Each practical application of the Law is evaluated through dialectical opposition, and the finer the discrimination that can be made to support a position, the better. Thought at its best is order and distinction, clarification. Daily life as lived according to principles of classification results in wholeness, completeness, that is, *shalom*.

Through such daily practices as food preparation or other sexually distinct social-ritual duties, "separation" becomes a principle inherent in thought and action. All items intended for a particular sex, whether toilet articles, clothing, or ritual garments, are forbidden to the opposite sex. During the Middle Ages, certain occupations, such as ritual slaughterer, and certain ritual practices, such as reading the Torah or wearing the prayer shawl, became defined by sex and prohibited to women.

The boundaries of the home are defined by the *mezuzah* ("doorpost"), the amulet on which are written a few words from Deuteronomy (6:4–9 and 11:13–21) and one of the mystical names of God. Like the blood on the doorposts of the Hebrews the night before the Exodus, the *mezuzah* defines the limits of the home and declares the identity of its occupants. The most pervasive system of separation, however, is found in the dietary laws. Foods are first defined as permitted (*kosher*, or "fit to eat") or prohibited (*trefah*).[1] Within the permitted category, further distinctions are made between dairy (*milchig*) and meat (*fleishig*) items, and those which are neutral and can be eaten with either meat or milk (*parveh*).[2] Time restrictions separate the consumption of the opposing categories, and strict rules govern the preparation of the foods. The dietary laws make dining with non-Jews very difficult, since foods, even those that are otherwise permitted, are prohibited if prepared by gentiles, unless a Jew has in some way assisted in the preparation. An apparently universal form of social communion, the sharing of wines, is impossible, since the Jew can only drink wines prepared and handled by Jews. Even in situations where Jew and gentile do eat together, the restrictions imposed on the Jew serve to remind him of his distinction. And if eating is made difficult and discouraged, sex or marriage with a gentile—the ultimate confounding of boundaries—can cause the Jew to be put outside the living society, to be considered dead.

The separated people are united with their God through the covenant, first established with Noah, accepted by Abraham, renewed

---

1. *Trefah*, which denotes any food forbidden by Jewish tradition, means specifically, according to the Torah, any animal killed by predators and any meat found diseased after slaughtering. *Nevelah* refers to any animal that has died of natural causes or through faulty ritual slaughtering.

2. *Milchig, fleishig*, and *parveh*, the most common terms referring to dairy, meat, and neutral categories, are Yiddish words.

collectively at Sinai, and reaffirmed each time a boy is circumcised. The concept of covenant indicates a two-way relationship between the Jew and God; it is a contract binding on both parties. The Israelites accepted the covenant at Sinai by agreeing to follow all the commandments of the Torah in exchange for God's favor and protection, and they demonstrated their acceptance by giving gifts to God in exchange for the "Pact" he placed in Moses' hands.[3] The word *brit* signifies both "covenant" and the ritual of circumcision itself.

If "covenant" indicates a reciprocal agreement, then either party can be held responsible for default. The prophets of the Bible, the rabbis of the Middle Ages, and even very traditional thinkers today have attributed the problems of Jewish existence to the failure of the Jews to fulfill their part in the covenant, that is, to ritual and moral laxity. Other Jews have followed the Hasidic rabbis of Europe, who railed at God, arguing that nothing the society could have done would ever have justified God's permitting massacres or the concentration camps. As bitter as the disappointment has been, it has taken place within the context of the covenant relationship. This belief is expressed in these words from eighteenth-century Russia:

Good morning, to You, Almighty God,
I, Levi Yitzhok son of Sarah of Berdichev,
Have come for a judgment against You,
On behalf of Your people Israel.
What do You want of Your people Israel?
Why do you afflict Your people Israel? . . .
From this spot I shall not stir,
I shall not stir from this spot,
There must be an end of this.
The exile must end!
Magnified and sanctified be His great name! [Ausubel and Ausubel 1957:97]

It is the reaffirmation of the covenant and not only the removal of the foreskin that constitutes the ritual of circumcision, the *Brit Milah* (Covenant of Inclination) or *Brit Abraham* (Covenant of Abraham). The entire ritual of the *brit*—its timing on the eighth day, the ritual official who performs the operation, the special words and actions, the mandatory drop of blood—is a public declaration that the child has been entered into the covenant and so may become a full member of Jewish society. The covenant with God separates the child from the gentile, a

3. "Pact" is the term used in the 1962 Jewish Publication Society translation of the Torah to refer to the stone tablets of the covenant at Mount Sinai.

distinction permanently marked by removing the foreskin. Among noncircumcised peoples, circumcision has long been the overt sign of separation, but even among populations that circumcise their males, the *brit* remains above all else the means through which Jewish society demonstrates to itself its unique relationship with God.

One effect of the covenant has been to stress man's responsibility for his social existence. In communities that have retained their integrity, whether in nineteenth-century eastern Europe or in twentieth-century New York City, the primary way of exhibiting responsibility has been through the acquisition of knowledge of the Law, and then by activating this knowledge in daily routine and in private and public ritual. The Seder can be seen as one remaining instance in which the extended community demonstrates its acceptance of the covenant by following a dictate from the Torah. However, even as the Seder is a demonstration and a reminder to the community of its obligations under the covenant, it is a reminder to God of his role in the welfare of the society. As the society shows its accord with rules set down in the past, it clears the way to deliverance.

The idea of a covenant through the Torah allowed the Jews to become a "priestly people," since they now had the means of knowing God's will. At Sinai, God says, "You shall be to me a kingdom of priests and a holy nation" (Exodus 19:6). Like the Law itself, the Jews are placed between God and man, becoming by example a "light unto all nations" (Isaiah 42:6).

Before the destruction of the Temple, it was the family of Aaron, the high priests or *kohens,* and the priestly tribe of the Levites, who took the greatest responsibility for upholding and demonstrating the laws of purity. Since 70 C.E., men have continued to take their tribal affiliation from their father, and many Jews today still trace their lineage to the priestly Levites and the *kohens,* or to one of the nonpriestly tribes, now collectively merged under the name Israel. While those of priestly lineage may retain some honors and functions in the synagogue, the responsibility for the Law has become more generally shared.[4] Where once the High Priest alone entered the Holy of Holies in the Temple on the Day of Atonement to repent the sins of the people, now all men repent the community's sins in collective prayer. Within the home, the man acts as priest, making certain that the instructions of the Torah are followed. Each meal has an aspect of formal ritual, proceed-

4. A rabbi is a "teacher," and not necessarily from a priestly line.

ing according to a strict code that emphasizes purity and separation. Hands are washed ritually before each meal, and benedictions are said before and after eating. Daily life is lived in agreement with rules that govern the most commonplace actions and keep the mind ever aware of the dichotomy between the sacred and the profane. The Code of Jewish Law describes in detail the correct way to put on shoes or to sleep at night.

The idea that the individual family has a responsibility for defining the whole as the "priestly people" can be seen in the ceremony of *Pidyon HaBen,* or Redemption of the First-born Son. In ancient times the first-born sons of all families, as well as the sons of the priests, were dedicated to the service of God.[5] When, in fact, not all these males were needed for service at the Temple or at altars elsewhere in the country, a ceremony was instituted to "redeem" the sons of the nonpriestly tribes from their obligation. This redemption takes place on the thirty-first day after the child's birth through a contribution to charity, given during the ceremony to a *kohen.*

The first-born's special relation to God is paralleled by the conception of the people Israel as the first-born son of God (Exodus 4:22). The idea of newness inherent in a first-born has been often seen to connote good fortune and special potency. When asked by the people of Jericho to purify the water, the prophet Elisha says, "Bring me a new cruse and put salt therein" (2 Kings 2:20). In Jewish magic of the Middle Ages, new things were used to ensure success, new cups, new swords, new clothing. One's fortune was understood to be connected to the first person one met in the morning, or the first action in the week, month, or year, and, as noted earlier, the pious Jew still blesses each new food he eats or new act he takes. The "first-born of a first-born" had especially potent magical associations in the Middle Ages, an idea that appears to have had its origin in the Bible.

"He who opens the womb" announces fertility, and in ancient times such new fertility was seen as a gift from God. In thankfulness, the first fruits of the harvest, as well as the first-born of the livestock, were given back to God at the altar. This appearance of a more active involvement by God in first births seems to make the relationship be-

5. "The Lord spoke further to Moses, saying, 'Consecrate to Me every first-born; man and beast, the first issue of every womb among the Israelites is Mine'" (Exodus 13:1–2). "When Pharaoh stubbornly refused to let us go, the Lord slew every first-born in the land of Egypt, the first-born of both man and beast. Therefore I sacrifice to the Lord every first male issue of the womb, but redeem every first-born among my sons" (Exodus 13:15).

tween God and the first fruits of man and nature more immediate; the first-born has an intermediate, indeed priestly, relationship between God and man. The individual's position—part of the family, yet at the same time elevated above it—is structurally congruent with the social definition of Jews as "a nation of priests." The protection of the first-born sons of the Israelites on the night of Passover foreshadows the collective assumption of first-born status at Sinai and the anointing of a first-born son, Aaron, as High Priest. In the Fast of the First-born on the morning before Passover, the first-born sons still retain a remnant of the ancient rite, when, like priests, they act for all men.

The creation in Exodus of a priestly people, the first-born of God, contains the ideas of both social separation and intermediate status. This intermediate status can take many forms. When consecrated, as in Exodus, it becomes priestly, but the same process of distinction that creates the priest can present problems in other planes of thought. Following God's command to be a "wise and discerning people" (Deuteronomy 4:6) also requires Jews to maintain the categorical distinctions so made. For this reason, all forms of ambiguity are suspect. There can be nothing that mediates—that is, reconciles or compromises—categorical boundaries. In Judaism, there are no saints or centaurs; and, following Leviticus 19:19, "You shall not let your cattle mate with a different kind; you shall not sow your field with two kinds of seed; you shall not put on cloth from a mixture of two kinds of material," hybrids in plant and animal life and the mixing of wool and linen *(sha-atnez)* are prohibited. Douglas attributes the logic of the dietary prohibitions to this need for categorical integrity (1970:54–72). Once the defining characteristics of the permissible animals are established, all items lacking these criteria immediately become taboo.

Even the prophet Elijah, a central figure in the Seder, is understood as a man who was raised to heaven alive. He is God's messenger on earth, but he is not divine; he is a bridge between two opposing states that reinforces the limits of each but does not merge them.

In accordance with the principle of absolute distinction, the priestly people are in an intermediate position between God and mankind, but they are not mediators who in any way reconcile opposites; rather, like the prophets, they are merely instruments through which God talks to all humanity. The priestly people are to be the means through which God's light comes to all nations. Similarly, a biblical prophet is not a diviner or a sorcerer, but only a mouthpiece for God: "I will put My words in his mouth and he will speak to them all that I command him" (Deuteronomy 19:18). The role of the priestly people is, like that of the prophet, to provide a clear channel through which God may speak to all peoples. But there are inherent problems, for, although God and his thoughts, as embodied in the words of the Torah, are perfect by definition, man is not, and he has trouble comprehending all the meanings of the words. Therefore, he must continually analyze and discuss the words, in order to articulate them in his actions.

The Jew's difficulty in complying with God's will is expressed through the character of Moses and through his faulty speech. God chooses Moses to be his spokesman before Pharaoh, a representative of all disbelieving nations, but Moses protests that he cannot provide a clear medium for God's words and refuses the responsibility:

> But Moses said to the Lord, "Please, O Lord, I have never been a man of words, either in times past or now that You have spoken to Your servant; I am slow of speech and slow of tongue." And the Lord said to him, "Who gives man speech? Who makes him dumb or deaf, seeing or blind? Is it not I, the Lord? Now go, and I will be with you as you speak and tell you what to say." But he said, "Please, O Lord, make someone else Your Agent." [Exodus 4:10–13]

Reluctantly, Moses assumes the role God has chosen for him, but only after God promises to allow Aaron to speak for Moses. God will speak directly to Moses, and Moses will tell Aaron what to say. Moses remains the intermediary, chosen to be in close relationship with God but imperfectly voicing God's words. He acts for God on earth, as when he lifts his arm at God's command and parts the Red Sea. But because he is impatient with God and with the people, because he momentarily lacks trust in God during the hardships of the desert, Moses loses the right to enter the Promised Land. The figure of Moses sums up the intermediate position of the priestly, imperfect people; Moses is the prototypical Jew.

Although mediation, as compromise, is impossible, transition is not. A state of transition implies having left one socially recognized state and not yet having reached another; it is a period of conversion, either quick, as in the revelation at Sinai, or slow, as in the gradual perfection of the Jew through the Law and his consequent approach to the Holy Land. Because transitional forms, like mediating ones, are "neither this nor that," they suggest ambiguity and thus danger. Implicit in the idea of transition is the concept of movement. As long as that movement goes forward toward a more positive state, "transition" can include an awareness of hope despite the perception of danger.

In his classic book *The Rites of Passage,* van Gennep used that phrase to indicate periods of transition between recognized social states, whether from child to adult or student to graduate (1969:10–11). The transition is usually described as beginning with the separation from the original status, a period of marginality, and then the final achievement of the new, non-threatening status. This process of becoming is often treated as a symbolic death and rebirth, and the completed transformation announced through visible acts appropriate to a new being, such as a new name and new clothing, and by acts such as loud noises that declare that the process is over and the ambiguous creature gone.

The culture that has valued order and distinction has also elaborated ways to transform items and individuals into members of other categories, to change the "unmarried man" at the wedding to a "married" state. Transformation is the result of imposing the products of the mind on social experience, and using acts or objects to indicate a change of basic nature and so suitability for a new category. Through the use of items seen to embody God's creative power—words, sacred objects —a completely "new" state is achieved.

Jewish thought has produced many such transformative acts and objects: words, time, and water are just a few of the means through which matter can be converted into a new state. In Exodus, the presence of God, revelation, transforms the Israelites from a wandering assemblage into a purposeful people with a law of their own. A "gentile" is a person without a Jewish mother, but socially defined agents of transformation, such as the pure waters of a ritual bath, and a ritual circumcision for a male, change the gentile into a Jew as valid as any. As is common in such transitions, a new name marks the new state of being: Avram becomes Abraham when he recognizes God, and the convert receives a new name when he or she becomes a Jew.

In all cultures, states of transition take on symbols of danger in recognition of their expression of non-order, declassification. In Jewish folk culture, childbirth, weddings, and death have been accompanied by a vast array of magical practices aimed at controlling the demonic forces that approach man when order appears to retreat. Such magic is "culture" of the interstices, the attempt to use socially recognized forms—words, objects, actions—in unusual ways in order to contain the chaos the system itself has created. This perception of extraordinary power, whether god or demon, is characteristic of transitional states.

The sense of threat that accrues to marginality also has to be considered when the people themselves are placed by their own system in an indeterminate state. The paradoxical result of the attempt of Jewish culture to create order through strictly defined categories has been to place Jewish society eternally in a transitional state between good and bad, between the promise of the covenant and its fulfillment, that is, to place it in the moral diaspora called the *galut.* And yet, such an in-between state, the state of the Hasid's *benoni* or intermediate man, includes not only the idea of danger but that of divine protection as well. Buber uses the term "holy insecurity" to describe this unusual state (1966:13).

It is in the story of the Exodus that all these concepts—distinction, ambiguity, transition, the covenant relationship, the priestly people—come together. It is at the Seder that the meanings are exchanged and made expressive of the experience of the individual Jew.

According to folk exegesis, the Seder is called to retell and celebrate, not re-enact, the convocation and sacrifice of the night before deliverance. By explicitly denying re-enactment, the moment before deliverance is placed once and for all time in the past, and the premise that the Jews have been eternally freed from their darkest hour is upheld. Yet the ritual necessarily has references that reach beyond the specific event, because, as symbolic form, the ritual is an inclusive system of relations that respond to historical context as well as to inherited tradition. "Jerusalem" as sign points to a particular city in the Middle East. "Jerusalem" as symbol, when placed in relation to its opposite, "Egypt," subsumes a range of allusions that link the biblical story with the social situation of the celebrants.

The social reality for the scattered communities that have developed the Seder as it is celebrated today includes their distance from the Promised Land. In a strictly historical sense, this means that any settlement outside the holy land is temporary. Like the Israelites in Egypt before the Exodus, Jews are "sojourners" in foreign lands. Even in countries where Jews are content and have no desire to leave, this sense of the non-realization of a goal is kept alive because of the other sense of "Jerusalem" as a moral destination, a place of reunification with God.

Although the diaspora Jew can meet God, as *Makom* ("Place") wherever or whenever he might seek him, the idea persists that God's true "home" is the Temple in Jerusalem. A rebuilt Temple in Jerusalem would place God in historical time, making possible the unity of the historical and the eternal—the messianic age of peace. As in Psalm 137,

"Jerusalem" becomes a symbol of the termination of the physical exile, a state that is necessarily, a moral exile also:

> By the rivers of Babylon,
> There we remembered Zion. . . .
> How shall we sing the Lord's song
> In a foreign land?
> If I forget thee, O Jerusalem,
> Let my right hand forget her cunning.
> Let my tongue cleave to the roof of my mouth,
> If I remember thee not;
> If I set not Jerusalem
> Above my chiefest joy.

"Jerusalem" has come to mean synthesis, wholeness, goodness, completeness, purity, perfect order, freedom, light, bodily resurrection, and eternal life. Even communities satisfied with residence outside of Israel continue to use the language of the Exodus. Repentance is called *tshuvah,* "return," and the words that close the Day of Atonement, Yom Kippur, are the same as those that close the Seder: "Next year in Jerusalem!"

By contrast, "Egypt" represents all that is alien, "otherness," as well as slavery, chaos, impurity, darkness, death and despair. Between these two polarities is the "desert," the period of wandering between Egypt and Jerusalem, the state between despair and hope. Whether one is in Egypt, the desert, or in Jerusalem is measured by one's distance from God in terms of fulfilling the obligations of the covenant. "Egypt" represents the ultimate distance: God has forgotten, the people are in darkness.

The story of Exodus highlights all the indeterminacies inherent in a state of transition as well as the great transformative moment at Sinai. Sometimes, however, no transformation between opposing categories of the culture is possible, and thus no transitional, or twilight, state can exist. This idea too is contained in Exodus, in the story of the passage of the Israelites across the Red Sea. The Israelites walk through on dry land; the Egyptians drown in the waters that close upon them.

In Jewish culture, immersion is a symbol of transformation from impure to pure. The Israelites have no need of such a transformation. Exodus tells how they groan in bondage and cry out:

> God heard their moaning and God remembered His covenant with Abraham and Isaac and Jacob. God looked upon the Israelites, and God took notice of them. [Exodus 2:24–25]

Here the primary responsibility for reactivating the covenant lies with the people, who must cry out and remind God of it. Once the link is reasserted, God's light shines on the Israelites, and separation from darkness, and from Egypt, begins. As darkness descends on Egypt, "all the children of Israel had light in their dwellings" (Exodus 10:23).

That deliverance, part of the process of reunification with God, begins with the Israelites' active concern for their earthly condition and their renewed recognition of God is expressed through the appearance of light in their homes while the rest of the world is dark and through the parting of the Red Sea. The parting of the Red Sea underscores the idea that the covenant that distinguishes the Israelite from the Egyptian was re-established prior to the departure from Egypt. The Israelites were not immersed in the waters of the Red Sea because transformation is not necessary. God closes the water on the Egyptians, and they drown, because transformation is impossible: to be "Egyptian" is to be "alien," forever the "other."

The image of a light coming from God to express God's relationship with the Israelites while the homes of all the Egyptians are dark is a use of the symbols of light and dark that pervades Jewish culture. Through ever-present, sensual experience, the positive and negative connotations of the Exodus are brought home each day. Light and dark have come to suggest God's presence or absence, freedom and slavery, Jerusalem and Egypt; a light brought into the darkness connotes the twilight or the transitional, desert state.

Probably first tied to the rising and setting of the sun, light and dark, as East and West, have given past and present communities ideal spatial orientation. In the Torah, east is the direction of the pure and innocent time of Eden, and the direction from which redemption will come. There is a legend that the eastern gate of Jerusalem will remain closed until the messiah comes. The wind that parted the Red Sea came from the east, as did the plague of locusts that God sent, and the Jews of the Exodus faced east as they traveled to the Promised Land.

Throughout daily life, reminders of the east continue to express hope and joy. Even at death, dirt from the Holy Land may be sprinkled on the coffin to symbolize the desired burial in the east. There was no prescribed orientation of bodies in cemeteries in Europe, in the Middle Ages, but frequently they were interred with their feet pointing toward the east, so that they could walk directly to the Holy Land when the messiah came.

One is always to face east when praying. In the home, a wall hanging, a *mizrah* ("east") hangs on the eastern wall to point the way. In the synagogue, the Ark of the Torah is placed in the eastern wall. Yet even this crucial compass point has become detached from its natural base. If it is physically impossible to locate the Ark in the wall facing east, the wall that houses the Torah automatically becomes the "eastern wall." And if "East" is joy, "West" carries with it ideas of despair.

Light and white represent all that is good and eternal: God, man's soul, purity. The early morning light in the east that erases the darkness suggests God at his most merciful, most approachable. Dawn is the time of redemption, when God delivered the Israelites from Egypt, and the time of day when dew and manna fell from heaven. It is also the favored time for individual prayer and for renewing the covenant at each circumcision. Phylacteries are put on at dawn, "when the first light of the sun is seen in the East" (Code of Jewish Law, vol. 1, 8:1).

In addition to natural daylight, God's presence is in the light in the fire and comes into each home regularly in the fire of the ceremonial candles.[6] On each Sabbath eve and on the eve of each festival candles are lit, thereby extending God's light into the darkness. At least two candles are lit, for the "double joy" of the day, but often a mother will light an additional candle for each child. This practice recalls the line from the Book of Proverbs: "The soul of man is the light of the Lord" (20:27). This idea is echoed in the tractate of the Talmud dealing with Passover, which equates the single candle with the soul of man (Pesahim 8a). In Europe, candles were burned beside the dead, and a candle is still burned on the anniversary of a parent's death. In some towns in Europe, after a burial it was customary to measure around the grave with wicking. The wick was later cut into pieces and made into candles to be burned in the synagogue in memory of the deceased. The State of Israel has adopted the candelabrum as its national emblem.

A single candle lights the searchers' way as they seek out the last bits of leaven the evening before Passover. That this is a ceremony and not a true search is demonstrated by the use of only a single candle, surely not light enough to uncover any truly hidden or overlooked leaven. As the family goes through the motions of seeking and gathering the "hidden" pieces of leaven, the single candle indicates the presence of God's light, as the soul of man, in the process of removing the forbidden and temporarily profane food.

In the Torah, God appears as a fire that does not consume, in the

6. As symbols of the eternal, ceremonial candles may not be used for the practical purpose of illumination.

burning bush[7] and at Sinai, and as a pillar of fire to give light to the Israelites at the Red Sea. In mystical thought, God is pure, white light which does not consume, and which man can never see. God's presence is seen instead in his emanations, the colors of the prism, each color expressing a different attribute of God, such as wisdom, insight, justice, and mercy (blue, green, red, and cream-white).

The idea of the eternal in fire was also seen in the fire at the altar in Jerusalem, and in the perpetual fire placed on the eastern wall before the Ark in many synagogues today. In some places, however, the fire is set as a light in darkness on the western wall.

God might also appear as consuming fire, which accepts, through smoke, matter offered him. Through contact with this fire, matter is transformed and purified. The Bible tells several times of a fire descending from heaven and consuming the offering on the altar (2 Chronicles 7:1-3). This process is duplicated in the woman's dedication of each loaf of bread to God by burning a "priestly portion" of the dough, in the burning of the leaven in the early morning hours before Passover, and in the purification of cooking utensils and ovens to be used for Passover by heating them until they glow.

The smoke of fire, like clouds, has been understood as a sign of communication between God and man. In the desert, smoke and clouds signified God's presence at Sinai and his protection over the ark of the Torah. At the Temple, incense was burned to send a pleasing odor to God amid the smoke ("Let my prayer arise like incense" [Psalm 141:2]), and all offerings to God were assured of sufficient smoke by placing fat or oil on the wood. On the High Altar of the Seder table, the flowers and candles combine sweet fragrance and smoke.

The relation between the white light of a fire that does not consume and consuming fire is expressed most completely in the mystical book of the Zohar ("Splendor"):

> Pursuing this idea, we may say that he who desires to penetrate into the mystery of the holy unity should contemplate the flame which rises from a burning coal or candle.
> There must always be some material substance from which the flame

7. The woman shields her eyes when pronouncing the benediction over the festival candles. Two reasons are given. Covering the eyes is said to recall Moses, who looked away from the burning bush when he realized God's presence within the fire. The second, legalistic reason is that a benediction must be said before the performance of the act. Since it is impossible to say the words over the light before kindling the candles, the woman first lights the candles, then covers her eyes, says the words, and looks on the light as if for the first time.

thus arises. In the flame itself may be seen two lights: the one white and glowing, the other black, or blue. Of the two, the white light is the higher and rises unwavering. Underneath it is the blue or black light upon which the other rests as on a support. The two are conjoined, the white reposing upon the throne of the black. The blue or black base is, likewise, connected to something beneath it, which feeds it and makes it cling to the white light above. At times this blue or black light turns red, but the light above remains constantly white. This lower light is in its nature an instrument for destruction and death, devouring whatever comes near it. But the white light above neither consumes nor demolishes, nor does it ever change.

   Therefore Moses said, "For the Lord thy God is a consuming fire" (Deuteronomy 4:24), consuming actually all that is beneath him . . . Moses stood in the supernal light, which does not consume and does not demolish. [Bereshit 50b–51a]

Consuming fire, then, mediates between the eternal—that which is transformed and purified—and matter that is left behind. As fire is heat and light and life, ashes are cold and dark and death. This relationship is in accord with the prohibition in Judaism against cremation of the dead. Death is understood as the process of separation of the warming life force, man's soul, from the body. Dead bodies, like ashes, are residue. Still, the doctrine of bodily resurrection has dictated that the body be treated with care, to be ready to receive its spiritual essence in messianic times.

Ashes are also used to suggest rebirth. Placed on the forehead of the mourner, they complement the symbolism of the eggs at the mourning meal. At weddings, following the tradition of eastern Europe, ashes are placed on the forehead of the groom, who wears a white *kittel,* as he begins his new life as a married man. And the pure white *kittel,* worn at death, at a wedding, and on the Day of Atonement, carries its associations of death and rebirth to the Passover Seder.

The *kittel,* then, is associated with periods of transition: death, the wedding, and the time of atonement. The prospective groom is separated from his former associates, goes through an ordeal of fasting, and then, dressed in white, assumes his married state. As on the Day of Atonement, the *kittel* represents a transitional state between the death of his old life and his new life as a married man, and suggests the purity of mind and heart with which he enters his new life. The *kittel* also suggests transition at the Seder, the ritual that celebrates a past transition and the transformation of a people. But the focus of attention at the wedding, Yom Kippur, and the funeral is not on past transformations but on present states of becoming. At the Seder also, the *kittel* refers to the current experience of the celebrants, not the past historical event.

The Seder is linked by its evening, early spring setting to the early fall penitential period of atonement, which begins on Rosh Hashana and culminates on Yom Kippur. The holidays are connected by their observance at transitional times in nature, and especially by two concepts: *tshuvah*—as the spiritual return to God that will make possible the physical return—and renewal. There are, in effect, two "new year's celebrations" in Jewish thought: the "official" New Year observance at Rosh Hashana ("Head" of the Year) on the first day of the seventh month, Tishri, and Passover, in the first month, Nisan. The rebirth of the society is celebrated at the time of the rebirth of the natural world. The Song of Songs is read at Passover, at the Seder and on the intermediate Sabbath of Passover in Ashkenazic communities,[8] because of its associations with spring and with the reawakened relationship between God and his people:

> For lo, the winter is past,
> The rain is over and gone;
> The flowers appear on the earth;
> The time of singing is come,
> And the voice of the turtle is heard in our land;
> The fig-tree putteth forth her green figs,
> And the vines in blossom give forth their fragrance,
> Arise, my love, my fair one, and come away. [2:11]

Passover has also been connected with the "New Year for Trees," *Tu B'Shevat,* the Jewish Arbor Day, celebrated on the fifteenth day of the month of Shevat with the planting of trees in Israel and, in the diaspora, by eating fruits grown in Israel. The kabbalists of Safed, Israel, developed an ordered service, a seder, for *Tu B'Shevat* based on the Passover Seder, a custom that has spread to Sephardic communities in Europe and North Africa.

Both Passover and the fall penitential period have similar symbolic forms: male ritual immersion may take place before each of them; the Seder and Yom Kippur conclude with the same words; both are occasions for family gatherings and festive meals; and the *kittel* is worn on both holidays. The death-to-life concepts conveyed by the ritual immersions and the *kittel* are reinforced at the Seder in the

8. If there is no intermediate Sabbath, the Song of Songs is read on the first day of Passover. In Sephardic communities, it is read before the afternoon service on the last day.

eastern European tradition by the presence of the separate plate of hard-boiled eggs. These additional eggs are not required by the Haggadah and are not part of most Sephardic Seders. Eggs are the only food required at a funeral, and the association with the time of death supports the transitional symbolism and serves to qualify the conscious joy of the evening.

The Haggadah openly reminds the participants of the transitional nature of the festival through the phrase "a night of watching." The Haggadah is described in popular literature as dealing with a liberation completed, but, in fact, it was developed by a population that saw itself in an indeterminate state, living precariously on the margins of society, awaiting deliverance. The "night of watching" of the historical Passover becomes, through its setting on a spring evening and other material forms, sensuously and cognitively united with the present:

> It is a night of watching unto the Lord for bringing them out of the land of Egypt: this same night is a night of watching unto the Lord for all the children of Israel throughout all their generations. [Exodus 12:42]

Convening the Seder at night makes the ritual consistent with concepts implicit in Jewish culture, and with exilic philosophy in particular. The Seder uses darkness and light to suggest the ideal oppositions Egypt and Jerusalem, as well as the twilight state of the present community. This twilight state, with all its possible gradations from despair to hope, is given a wide latitude for expression through the ritual exchange.

The exile in Europe and wherever else Jews have lived outside of the Promised Land has found its explanation through the metaphor of the Exodus, a state of wandering with the Torah as a guide.[9] Exile, in its simplest form, implies distance from God, but exile can have an even harsher connotation, that of willful disobedience and God's subsequent punishment. This is the view expressed in one of the many transformations of the Exodus story, that in the Book of Ezekiel. After the fall of the first Temple in Jerusalem in 586 B.C.E., the prophet Ezekiel went with the Israelites who were exiled to Babylonia. Like Jeremiah, who stayed behind, Ezekiel uses the language of Exodus:

> I lifted up My hand unto them also in the wilderness, that I would scatter them among nations, and disperse them through countries; because they had not executed Mine ordinances. [Ezekiel 20:23]

9. The black Jews of Ethiopia, the *Beta Yisrael,* are commonly called "Falashas," an Amharic word meaning "immigrants" or "exiles."

... Thus saith the Lord God: Behold, I will take the children of Israel from among the nations, whither they are gone, and will gather them on every side, and will bring them into their own land; and I will make them one nation in the land. [Ezekiel 37:21–22]

Moreover I will make a covenant of peace with them . . . it shall be an everlasting covenant with them; and I will establish them, and multiply them and will set My sanctuary in the midst of them forever. My dwelling place shall be over them; and I will be their God, and they shall be My people. [Ezekiel 37:26]

Exile in Babylonia and exile in Europe are analogous. They are not Egypt, because the Torah exists, but through his own fault, the Jew can come very close to living in a state of darkness and slavery.

When the Exodus is perceived as past event, the sequence slavery-wilderness-freedom is acknowledged. But when the Exodus story acts as an explanatory device for present-day reality, the distinction between slavery and wilderness almost disappears, and slavery-wilderness appears as the binary opposite of freedom. The present state of moral imperfection and distance from land and God becomes close to being the oppressive opposite of the messianic days.

In more recent times, the imagery of Exodus has been applied to the mass emigration of Jews to America. America was looked upon as the Promised Land by many emigrants from eastern Europe, and this idea conflicted with the traditional understanding of Palestine as the land of freedom. After the Second World War, the migration of Jews from Europe to Palestine was likened to the biblical story; one boat of refugees trying to run the British blockade was named the *Exodus*. The departure of Jews from the Soviet Union, and from other countries where life is considered difficult, is fit into the Exodus framework.

One place above all has come to represent the *galut* state of the diaspora Jew, between darkness and light. Throughout the years, pilgrims from all over the world have come to pray for deliverance from physical and moral exile at the Western, or "Wailing," Wall in the city of light, Jerusalem. The wall is believed to be the last remaining wall of the ancient Temple. Because of its location in Jerusalem, the wall brings together all the concepts of joy and despair, East and West, and has acted as a tangible symbol of the aspirations of the people of the exile.

The perception of the conditions of the *galut* gave rise to increased speculations about the nature of the man who would come to end it.

Before the destruction of the second Temple and the subsequent dispersion of the people, there had been little discussion of the character of the messiah or the conditions of the "World to Come," although the ideas are found in the Torah. In Exodus, God himself is the redeemer, and elsewhere, as in the Book of Daniel, the whole Jewish people will act as their own messiah. Concepts of the messiah, in particular, but also of the golden age yet to come, were more fully developed after the defeat of the armies of Bar Kochba by the Romans and the fall of the second Temple. The Jewish state had been conquered before, but the conquest had usually been some form of political containment, and some degree of religious expression was still possible. The new Roman occupation, which prohibited religious activity, also generated new development of messianic ideas.

In the Talmud, two conceptions of the means to end the dispersion of the Jews were developed. One stresses the moral failings of the people and urges the erasure of sin and the performance of charitable acts in order to hasten redemption. In this view, the messiah, who will eventually be sent by God, will be a gentle, peaceful man descended from the ancient king of Israel, David. Concurrently, another type of messianic figure is envisioned, a heroic warrior who will succeed where Bar Kochba failed, the Messiah ben Joseph, who will lead a victorious war against the forces of evil and restore the Jews to their land. This "political messiah" will die in battle once his mission is completed, and the messianic days of peace will be ushered in by the "gentle messiah."

The messianic concepts describe two facets of one ideal human: physically and spiritually strong and able to triumph over evil on both political and moral planes, but ultimately ruled not by his physical strength but by his wisdom and morality. Although identified as "of the house of David" and "of Joseph," the messiahs have no names and are themselves unimportant except as personifications of the future and role models for man.

As there are two conceptions of the messiah, there are also two conceptions of the time when he will come. One theme stresses the advent of the messianic days after a gradual and conscious self-perfection by the community. In the other, a "miracle" occurs: the messiah comes just when everything seems darkest, just as God delivered the Israelites when the sufferings of slavery in Egypt were greatest. In the first conception, the people make their own miracle; in the second, God intrudes into history to work the change. Both ideas are woven throughout the actions and imagery of daily life and the Seder and serve as expressions of the responsibility of both man and God for bringing the messiah.

The ideas of the character and advent of the messiah appeared to be realized in 1648 when the most notable of the "false messiahs," Sabbetai Zevi, declared himself the deliverer. This was not the first time that a "false messiah" had capitalized on the people's yearnings for the end of the exile. However, the intelligent, charismatic Sabbetai Zevi's cause was supported by legend and pain: in folk accounts the messiah's birth was connected to the date of the destruction of the Temple, the ninth of Av, Sabbetai Zevi's birthday, and Sabbetai Zevi seemed to fulfill the prediction of a messiah who would come when everything was darkest. Jewish existence in Europe had been precarious for many years, and the troubled times increased speculation among the mystics about the exact date of the coming of the messiah. The year they settled on was 1648. That date also marks the beginning of the decade of Ukrainian peasant revolts started by Chmelnitzki, which brought widespread death and destruction in eastern Europe; over one hundred thousand Jews perished during this period. To many, Sabbetai Zevi's appearance seemed divinely ordained. A wave of messianism spread throughout Europe; people sold their possessions and gave up their occupations in preparation for the return to Jerusalem. Their hopes turned to despair when it became apparent that Sabbetai Zevi could not fulfill his promises, and he converted to Islam in his native Turkey.[10] But "false messiahs" such as Sabbetai Zevi can appear only when the concept of the true messiah, whether sent by God or realized through human will, is kept alive. The Seder is imbued with ideas of messianic deliverance.

It is consistent with the meanings of the Seder to hold it at night, at the blackest time. It may seem only logical to inaugurate the Passover festival in the evening, since in Jewish calculation the day begins at sunset, and all Jewish holidays are observed from sunset to sunset. But there is a slightly different situation on Passover when the meal is preceded by a lengthy ritual and, unlike the meal on the Sabbath or Rosh Hashana, dinner cannot be eaten until quite late in the evening. The last meal containing leaven has been breakfast, and only a light lunch is eaten because everyone is occupied with holiday preparations. The time between lunch and dinner becomes a semi-fast, and for the

10. The descendants of some of Sabbetai Zevi's followers who also converted to Islam live today as the Donmeh sect of Turkey.

young, especially, this turns the Seder into something of a trial. Coming after weeks of strenuous household activities, the festival described by the males in the abstract terms of "Festival of Freedom" and "Festival of Joy" is not uncommonly referred to as a "joyous ordeal" by the women and children. This does not deny their pleasure at being together with family and friends to celebrate the greatest event in Jewish history. It does, however, recognize a side of Passover the writers of the traditional chronicles, all men, ignore.

Convening the Seder at night recalls the historical account, which places the first Passover meal at night. But night, black, the absence of light, has also been used to suggest moral imperfection. The darkest time of night has been understood as the expression of exile, when moral blackness mirrors nature's blackness, and the time when God is most likely to hear the prayers of the righteous, as he heard the cries of the Israelites in darkest Egypt. In the Middle Ages pious men, dressed in black, would rise at midnight to read a special liturgy that describes the destruction of the Temple and the dispersion of the people.[11] Seated on the floor, they confessed the sins they felt might be delaying the coming of the messiah. With dawn would come redemption. The Haggadah tells of five rabbis who studied the holy books through the night, until the early morning light came. And at the conclusion of the first Seder, the reading, "And it Came to Pass at Midnight," tells of all the miracles that God has performed for the Jews, just when everything seemed blackest.

The image of the table as the High Altar sums up the present and eternal coordinates of Jewish community. Each household becomes a miniature Jerusalem in exile. Presiding over the table, the father assumes the role of High Priest. Regardless of his status outside the home, his learning, his wealth, or tribal heritage, tonight he is supreme as the leader of the community assembled before him. He has come from the ritual bath; he sits in a white robe before a white tablecloth. Flowers and candles are on the table before him; each dish and wine glass is whole, unblemished; and his family, friends, and perhaps a Jewish stranger form his congregation.

When the leader, representing all the family, takes his seat at the Seder, he looks toward the dawn, the East. If possible, he sits facing the door through which the most honored guest of all will enter: Elijah, God's messenger. Even if the actual room precludes such orientation,

11. The fast of the Ninth of Av, commemorating the destruction of the Temple and other tragic events, is called the Black Fast.

he and all the community at the Seder will turn to face that door when Elijah is welcomed. By definition, the forerunner of the messiah comes from the East, and so the door is always in the east. By complying with God's directives to hold the Seder, each family metaphorically opens the door to the East Gate of Jerusalem.

4
The Setting

I am my beloved's, and my beloved is mine . . .
The Song of Songs

The setting of the Passover ceremony is the most significant statement of the Seder's central place in Jewish life and the key to understanding its ability to command loyalty. The Seder takes place in the home, at night, in the early spring, and each factor in its setting contributes to the dense network of meanings that constitute the ritual. Both place and time work to give the cognitive structures of society, as played out in Exodus, the emotional base needed to make them an intrinsic part of daily action.

The home and the synagogue have been the two arenas for enacting the prescriptions of the Torah and Talmud, and the actions in each support and validate the other. However, despite the importance of the home, it is in the synagogue, the "house of study," that activities conveying the highest social honor take place. Many holidays such as the Sabbath have their important home rituals, but the activities of the synagogue have been understood to be of equal or greater value. It is only on Passover that the ritual focus shifts to the home. While Passover has its synagogue observances, it is the Seder, with its text, its mingling of ages and sexes, its concern with the unlearned, and its sensual appeal, which has become the more important observance. Understanding why this is so requires a close examination of the values and meanings suggested by the concepts "home" and "community," as well as a consideration of the social and symbolic roles of men and women.

The Jewish home can best be described as a "home within a home." The boundaries of the physical home are marked by *mezuzahs* on each

47

doorway. Each time he passes across a threshold and touches his hand first to the name of God and the sacred words in the amulet, and then to his lips, the person is brought into direct contact with the concept that separation is godly. The division and distinction between home and outside is realized and reinforced, and the home assumes the aspect of a sanctuary. The idea of sanctuary is centered on the dinner table, which, through a complex of regulations attendant on it, has become understood as an altar in exile.

Before the fall of the second Temple, there were local altars for offerings wherever a group resided, although at major festivals sacrifices were brought to the High Altar in Jerusalem. These altars provided asylum; the fugitive supplicated God by grabbing the horns of the altar, its most sacred part. At Passover, instead of a lesser altar, the dinner table becomes the High Altar of the Temple in Jerusalem, and exhaustive preparations in compliance with stringent laws are necessary for its creation.

The new paint, dishes, and clothes and the thorough cleaning of the home in the weeks before Passover renew the home as nature outside renews itself. The change that takes place in the home is like the purification of a temple rather than a transition from profane to sacred. The home always has rituals that consecrate it, such as candle lighting and the dietary laws, and meals always require ritual hand washing and benedictions. When, however, the home is to house the High Altar, special preparations are needed. Since in ancient times the High Altar had to be perfect and the priest free of physical deformity and of irreproachable moral character, for the present reconstruction of the Temple there must be no dirt, blemishes, or impurities in the home.

To a very great extent, the woman in the home is responsible for the care of the table-altar through her preparation of food, although the man presides by delivering the benedictions before the meal. Because of the importance of dietary regulations to the entire Jewish conceptual system, and because of other ritual duties performed within the home, the home and the woman who manages it are seen as essential to the success of the extended home, the community.

The boundaries of the community are just as clearly defined as the individual home, with the idea of sanctuary implicitly extended. Instead of a *mezuzah* with God's name on it, there is the comprehensive system of rules enacted in God's name. For the observant, the rules mark the absolute limits to which a Jew can go and still remain part of the community. Because these rules are understood to articulate God's plans for the daily life of his select people, acting within these rules makes life holy and a sanctified haven against the outside world.

The concern with the idea of community in Judaism cannot be overemphasized. "Judaism" itself is derived from the name of a tribe, Judah, and not of a god or leader. Another common term for the extended community, *Bet Yisrael,* is more exactly translated "the house," or "family," of Israel. "Israel" here is the name of the collective, as well as the name of the ancestor; home, kin, and community are the same.

The focal point for the strivings of the community has always been the Temple in Jerusalem, which has represented temporal and spatial unity in physical form. As the place where man meets the god whose laws dictate daily life, "Temple," as ideal or past structure, brings together the contingent, historical, and varied experiences of man with the eternal.

After the fall of the Temple and the general dispersion, the local synagogue and the home came to share the functions of the Temple. The synagogue is primarily a house of study and communal prayer, and in communities that follow the traditional separation of the sexes, a house of male assembly. Because it is here that the laws which control the society are studied and debated, the synagogue has also served as the political and social center of the community.

It is in the home, however, that the transformation from "nation" to "community" has been realized for the now landless people. "Nation" depends on territory for its meaning, and, until recently, the idea of territory remained a dream. In the meantime, "community," bound by eternal laws not tied to a physical entity, has replaced "nation" as the ideal representation of the Jews. "Community" is a concept that allows the people to see themselves as united despite the loss of the land and outside the conventions of time and space. The synagogue has elaborated the laws that give the community this eternal definition, but the laws have been tied to an emotive, familial base in the home.[1]

The Law has worked to make "society" a paramount good, given its *raison d'être* by God. Society is viewed as an organism, and an illness in one part of the body—nonobservance of the rules by one person— weakens it all. For instance, while rules are sometimes relaxed when illness threatens an individual's life, one should die rather than publicly

1. The establishment of the State of Israel has not materially changed this perception. Through the Law of Return, all Jews may become citizens of Israel, but the assumption of Israeli nationality is a more limiting concept than "community" and only a partial, physical solution to the problem of exile.

violate certain tenets of the Law in a manner that might set an example for others and so weaken the bonds of society. This self-denial in order to maintain the integrity of Judaism and of the community is called *Kiddush HaShem,* Sanctification of the Name.[2] In the section of the Seder dealing with the four types of sons, the one called "wicked" is the one who excludes himself from the laws of the community.

The concern with the wholeness of society and its perfection and the identity of the individual with the whole are reflected in the treatment of the body. Like the society of which it is a part, the body must be kept clean and unblemished, and mutilation through incision or tattooing is prohibited. The body is the house of God on earth, and as such it must be respected and protected: "One shall not mortify the body; 'he who does harm to his body does harm to his soul' " (Buber 1966:126). Through periodic immersion in a ritual bath, the individual demonstrates his respect for God's creation, as he does in his everyday care of his body. A legend from the Talmud sums up this idea. When Rabbi Hillel was asked why he considered washing his body a pious deed, he replied, "If a man who is appointed to wash and polish the statues of kings receives not only payment for his work but is even regarded as among the great ones of the realm, how much more important is it that I keep my body, created in the divine image, clean" (Trattner 1955:76).

The subordination of the individual to his community is re-emphasized at various junctures in his life. After birth, the procedures governing the boy's public incorporation into the social and historical-religious ancestral community at the circumcision ceremony take precedence over any other ritual observance, including those of the Sabbath and Day of Atonement. In the Middle Ages communal wedding rings, borrowed from the synagogue for the occasion, emphasized the local society's participation in each marriage, while the ceremony itself stressed the broader concept of community. Even burial must take place in land set aside and consecrated by the whole: the public cemetery is the second requirement of a new settlement; the ritual bath, the means of insuring the community's purity, is the first.[3]

Within the synagogue, all prayers in the liturgy are expressed in

2. During World War II many Jews lived as Christians in order to hide from the Nazis. This was permitted as long as one adopted papers, not practices.

3. One of the first community associations formed by Jewish immigrants to America around the turn of the century was the burial society, whose purpose was to insure the proper treatment of the dead. Women joined sewing circles to make ritually correct shrouds for the community.

the plural. Even the penitential prayers of the Rosh Hashana and Yom
Kippur are statements of collective guilt. Personal prayer is possible at
any time, but in many situations, formal public prayer requires the
presence of at least ten men. Since such public devotions are obligatory for the observant Jew, each man in an Orthodox community feels
the responsibility to attend services if only to facilitate the obligations
of others. Heilman discusses this process of mutual responsibility and
the resultant interaction among the Orthodox in *Synagogue Life*
(1973), but even nonobservant men will often recognize this obligation
and attend prayer meetings if asked to be the "tenth man." (Recent
attempts in America to allow women to be counted in the *minyan* ["a
number," or "a few"; that is, a quorum] have met with varying de-
grees of success.)

It has always been understood that salvation comes to the individual Jew through the moral perfection of the community and not on his
own merits alone. Therefore, the individual has an active interest in
seeing that the social rules are maintained by others, and he understands his own accomplishments or failures as contributing to the early
or late arrival of the messiah. Similarly, the core value of *tzedakah* is
understood not as "charity" but as "social justice." It is a principle of
mutual obligation that serves to mitigate social inequalities in a society
that otherwise allows distinctions based on learning, wealth, or ancestral or tribal background.

This obligation to others was an everyday part of Jewish life in
Europe and is still in many traditional homes. Ritual actions are accompanied routinely by a coin put into a charity box. In densely populated
communities, representatives of charitable organizations travel from
home to home, collecting this change and linking the homes through
recognition of charity as a social obligation. On a larger scale, appeals
for funds through the mail or at fundraising dinners are an ever-present
part of Jewish society today, and the success of these appeals indicates
the persistence of the concept of *tzedakah* even when other beliefs
wane.

In daily life, the dietary rules and laws of endogamy preclude other
than necessary economic social intercourse with gentiles, and the individual is dependent on community support to meet his ritual obligations. In most Orthodox communities, the internal demands of prayer,
kosher food, and ritual bath combine to limit the degree to which the
individual can stray. In the ultraorthodox centers of the Hasidim, the
individual is further separated from outside society through educational

and socialization systems that do not prepare him for life away from the group.

It is in the routine and repetition of daily life that laws become common-sense actions and perspectives, and it is in the home that legal principles are refracted through emotive and sensual means that make their implementation a natural part of life. It has been the woman, with her obligations of child rearing, candle lighting, cooking, and cleaning, her folk tales and folk songs, who has been the primary instrument of transmission of the basic assumptions about the nature of the Jewish universe. No matter what might be her other activities—many women in eastern Europe ran small businesses—these duties were hers.

If the home was the heart of the community, the woman has been the heart of the home. "A man's home is his wife," says the Talmud (Yoma I, i), and the Code of Jewish Law concurs: "A man should ever be careful to treat his wife with respect, for it is only for the wife's sake that a man's house is blessed" (vol. 4, 145:10). At the wedding, the groom stands with his bride under a canopy *(huppah)*, suggestive of the home. The bride "encompasses" the groom as she is led several times around him. One explanation for this custom is that it acts out the phrase in Jeremiah 31:22 that says, "A woman shall court [go around] a man." Although in different traditions the number of circles varies from two to thirteen, seven is the most common number because, according to another explanation, as she encircles him, the bride enters the seven spheres of her new husband's soul. Still another explanation, and one certain not to please feminists, is that by so encircling him, the bride implies acceptance of the bridegroom as the "center of her universe" (Sperling 1968:282). The circle is also said to symbolize the aura of light in which marriage envelops a man.

The married state is a necessary and honored one in Judaism, and the Talmud suggests that a man be married at least by the time he is twenty, so that he shall be able to fulfill his primary commandment, "to be fruitful and multiply." For this *mitzvah*, he needs a wife, since intercourse outside of marriage is a sin. But sex within marriage may be for more than procreation. The Torah, Talmud, the Code of Jewish Law, and other rabbinic writings repeatedly make reference to a man's obligation to "rejoice" his wife, and the Torah exempts a newly married man from military service so that he may be with his wife (Deuteronomy 24:5). The Seven Blessings of the Marriage Ceremony from the Talmud (Ketubot 8a) describe the desired state of marriage. They begin with the blessing over the wine, acknowledge completeness when male and female are married, express hope for the end of the exile, exalt man's procreative power, and end with three blessings that thank God for the married state. The final two are:

> Blessed art Thou, O Lord our God, King of the universe, who hast created joy and gladness, bridegroom and bride, mirth and exultation, pleasure and delight, love, fellowship, peace, and companionship.

> Soon may there be heard again in the cities of Judah and in the streets of Jerusalem, the voice of joy and gladness, the voice of the bridegroom and the voice of the bride, the jubilant voice of bridegrooms from their marital canopies and of youths from their feasts of song. Blessed art Thou, O Lord, who causest the bridegroom to rejoice with the bride.

As "wife" and "woman" can only have meaning in relation to "husband" and "man," so "home" and "synagogue" describe spheres of action that can only be defined in the total web of the culture. While defining these separate spheres for the woman and man, Jewish culture also emphasizes their interdependence. Each sphere lacks complete autonomy because an interpenetrating system of symbols binds them together. As the female is dependent on the male for his knowledge and administration of the Law, so the male cannot "reach God" and implement the Law without the cooperation of a willing wife.

The interdependency of male and female is expressed in a number of talmudic writings, but is perhaps best summed up in this story of the charismatic leader of the Hasidic movement, the Baal Shem Tov (the Master of the Good Name). The Baal Shem Tov believed that, like Elijah, he would rise up to Heaven in a storm. When his wife died, he said: "I thought that a storm would sweep me up to Heaven like Elijah. But now that I am only half a body, this is no longer possible" (Buber 1975:82).

The rationalist tradition in Judaism has emphasized the ordering power of categorical distinction; the mystical tradition has recognized the distinctions but has attempted to go beyond them to bring resolution. Both systems have operated concurrently in the culture, and in many instances the mystical acts not as a separate system, but as an enrichment of conceptions already present in talmudic and biblical literature. The Book of Isaiah, for example, contains portions suggestive of a female-male relationship between the community and God ("For the Lord hath called thee,/As a wife forsaken and grieved in spirit;/And a wife of youth, can she be rejected? . . ." [54:6]). This relationship has been developed in mystical writings into rather overt sexual imagery that suggests the union of opposites, on both the familial and divine planes. If the mystic goes further along the path than the rationalist, still he often starts at the same point.

The male-female relationship in Judaism will be examined first according to the polarities of the rationalist model, and then the mystical extensions of these ideas will be explored in order to understand how the home can appear as the symbol of an ideal, a holy synthesis in a culture that otherwise deplores the blurring of boundaries.

The anthropological concepts of "nature" and "culture" are useful in elucidating the female-male relationship in Judaism. As discussed above, "culture" indicates the attempt to order and control experience through the imposition of the mind on it; the transformation from the unprocessed, "natural" state to the "cultural" state is expressed in Lévi-Strauss's simple metaphor of the raw and the cooked. To be "cooked" is to be changed in a way consistent with and expressive of the inherent principles of thought that govern the manifestation of all social forms.

While powerful in organizing the symbolic matrices that accrue around each word, the distinctions "nature" and "culture" tend to emphasize the polarities and not the symbiotic ties that bind the Jewish universe. Culture, in the general sense, is the push and pull of categorical distinctions and the attempt at resolving them through encompassing symbols, either informally in daily life or formally in public ritual. Terms in opposition to one another, such as "nature" and "culture," "dominant" and "subordinate," "active" and "passive," describe systems of relationships whose members depend on their partners for their own meaning, much as Mead's "Self" cannot be defined without reference to the "Other." Dominance is a relative and not an absolute concept; the "dominance" of the male in society can be compromised according to the powers attributed to the female, and these powers, in turn, may vary with the social situation or the ideological filter through which they are viewed.

The investigation of the relationship between the sexes through the medium of the structuralist framework reveals the complexity of the term "nature" when applied to Jewish social materials. "Nature" refuses to stay categorized as that which is dominated; its meaning as that which is undifferentiated and continuous becomes paramount. As will be demonstrated later, this conception of the natural world as a space or location undisturbed by time makes "nature" a term suggestive of a universe that man may dominate but that may in turn dominate him, in other words, nature as Divine Principle. The female in

Judaism, by her symbolic alliance with the "nature" pole of the continuum, suggests this dual relationship with "culture."

In its simplest form, to understand the relationship between "man" and "woman" according to the concept of "culture" is to place the sexes along a scale that measures their degree of involvement in the cognitive ordering that governs society. In one sense, all human beings are creators and creations of "culture," since the roles and rules they follow are the products of collective consensus. The terms "man" and "woman" are symbolic elaborations on basic biological distinctions; the beliefs about the inherent attributes of the sexes may or may not retain a connection with physical distinction. One gets one's concepts of how to perform even the most "natural" of bodily processes through one's culture, and these rules of social behavior with their implied values and perspectives are, in turn, transmitted to the young by both men and women. Still, if the degree of control over "nature" as untransformed matter is used as the key to the distinction between the sexes, then men appear to be more allied with "culture" and women closer to, but not part of, "nature."

The position the woman has held in Judaism is a specific instance of the woman's social situation in many societies. The female's biological functions have been used to connect her with social roles that cast her as instrument, and not administrator, of "culture's" rules. Primarily, she has been the guardian of the young, those not fully aware of society's laws, as well as nurse to the elderly or ill, those often exempt from the most stringent applications of the Law. Because of her necessary preoccupation with human biological needs, which limit or preclude her participation in the larger social arena where the activities of social control, public policy and law take place, the perception of the woman as a fully "cultural" being is compromised.

Although the "charter" for the society, the Torah, is understood as having been given to the total community, in practice it has been in the stewardship of the men. The men have been the "high level" interlocutors between God and humanity, the priests who study, interpret, and transmit the Torah as "divine culture." In Judaism, "culture"-making is divine process: implementing the divine order implies comprehending it first, and so attempting to reach the mind of God. The closer the man comes to that goal, the more he is satisfied that he is correctly articulating the Law, the more God-like is his role in society, and the further he is separated from the female.

The concept of time has been used throughout Jewish culture to mark distinctions between "nature" and "culture," and so to reinforce social roles. Time binds society and defines its purpose. As a community separated from surrounding populations, Jewish society has a consecrated mission located in historical time, with a moment of creation at Sinai and a messianic resolution in the future. In the culture, management of time is control, a means of limiting the boundless, and of giving distinction and meaning to the endless repetition of daily life. The festivals of Passover, Shavuot, and Sukkot were once, as agricultural celebrations, tied to changes in nature, but each acquired meanings and a code of time-dictated actions with only a loose or arbitrary connection to natural phenomena. In the southern hemisphere, the festivals are observed along with the rest of world Jewry although the seasons are reversed. Passover's Fast of the First-born, the Search for the Leaven, the Seder, *use* natural phenomena such as the rising or setting of the sun to express cultural meanings, but it is the culture that is imposing its definition on nature and not the other way around. Setting aside the seventh day for rest is a "cultural" step used each week to "stop time" itself. As the "day of holy unity," it is a period when temporal and eternal times are synthesized.

The man's life is structured by considerations of time. He is obligated to perform a daily round of private and collective prayer, starting with private meditations early in the morning and continuing through the day with the synagogue's three communal prayers in the morning, afternoon, and early evening. The Sabbath and major festivals are marked by extra, obligatory prayers in the synagogue. These requirements of communal prayer influence the conduct of daily life. Home and work must be accessible to the synagogue, and work must allow for these necessary interruptions for prayer.

The woman in the home is much less structured by time. She must, of course, be aware of time in her daily preparation and separation of food, and in preparations for the Sabbath and other festivals, especially Passover. And, of course, she is tied to the grand clock of the menstrual cycle and the prescriptions of menstrual purity. She is freed, however, from the absolute schedule of daily prayer that controls the man. Her obligations that relate to time—ritual immersion or candle lighting—come less frequently than his, and on a daily basis, she can manipulate her timed obligations. This less rigorous schedule leaves her freer to carry out her role as caretaker of the child.

The "child" is one who is not fully "enculturated," not fully aware of the rules of the society. "Child" also implies a non-mastery of natural impulses, an inability to subordinate either biological demands or will to the requirements of a schedule such as the daily, weekly, or yearly round of obligatory ritual performances that govern the man, or not yet subject to the less frequent menstrual rules that pattern the woman's life. The child therefore cannot be held to fixed rules and time constraints, and is freed from responsibility for failure to implement the Law in his daily life. Aside from the Seder, the child is not part of any social ritual, except as a passive "object" at the circumcision and at the Redemption of the First-born. His position at the Seder is that of one learning the rules and beliefs of the society, and even then, his role may be taken instead by an adult if no child is present.

The child, then, is "untimed," and the man "timed." The woman is somewhere in between, more constrained than the child, more flexible than the man. In this sense she is midway between child and man, "nature" and "culture." This positioning is recognized at the Seder: when there is no child to read the Four Questions, a woman is the first choice for a substitute.

Jewish society has elaborated the biological distinctions of male and female through the processes of incorporating the boy and girl into adult society, the adult being understood as one who is responsible for his actions. The boy's rites of passage are based on progressive separation from his "natural" state. When he is eight days old, he is made part of the social universe by having a natural part, the foreskin, removed from the area of his body that, at the time, is all that identifies him as male. Until recent years, the foreskin retained its association with the natural world by being returned to the earth, either by being buried or by being placed in dirt or sand. At the circumcision, the boy receives his social definition—his name—in a way that links him to the larger society through the male line. He becomes Abraham Yitzhak ben Yaacov HaLevi—Abraham Isaac, son of Jacob the Levite—an individual, part of a nuclear family, part of the extended tribal family.

Although all members of the community may attend the *brit,* the ceremony is the responsibility of the males. It is the duty of the father to have his son circumcised, and the ritual circumciser, the *mohel,* is considered to be acting in the father's stead. The child first meets "culture," in the words and actions of the *mohel,* as he is being separated from his natural state.

As a result of this ceremony, the boy now has a right to participate in public rituals such as the Seder. Although in Jewish law a child is Jewish if his mother is Jewish, he remains a "natural" member of the community unless transformed into a "cultural" being at the *brit*. Uncircumcised, he is a marginal being, an *aral*. [4]

At three or four, the boy in a very traditional family is removed from his home for most of the day to begin his studies in the Law. With a bit of sugar on his lips, or candy showered on his head to indicate the sweetness of learning, he goes to the synagogue, where his socialization is taken over by men for much of the day. At this age it is assumed that he has mastered his most basic biological demands, and is ready for mastery of the "culture."

By thirteen, the boy becomes an adult by demonstrating his knowledge of the Law before a public forum in the synagogue. He becomes a "man of duty," a *Bar Mitzvah*, for the rest of his life. Although *Bar Mitzvah* is commonly translated "son of the commandment," the Aramaic word *bar*, like *ben* in Hebrew, connotes age, membership in a class, or the possession of a particular quality, a change of status. As *ben* at the circumcision announces the child's new status as a member of the community as well as his familial relationship, *bar* at thirteen announces his transformation into an adult. As a *Bar Mitzvah*, the youth may now be counted as part of a *minyan*, the group of ten men necessary for worship, and he may now lead a Seder. With the assumption of adult privileges comes the vulnerability to sin, for with ritual and social responsibility comes the possibility of failure. A few years later he may marry.

The synagogue takes on the attributes of a "the men's house," and is the place where the boy learns to participate in his most valued activity, the quest for God through study of the Torah. Intellectual virtuosity is stressed; emotion is a by-product of rational processes of debate and understanding. Knowledge implies more than familiarity with the teachings; it is the demonstration of the ability to splice meanings and so comprehend and construct the order revealed in God's Law. Through knowledge the boy verifies his manhood and gains the right to participate in administering the rules that control society.

In each case, it is the society's decision about the time of maturity, not the boy's actual physical or mental condition, that determines his progress. He is fitted into established categories of "child" and "adult."

4. A child cannot be circumcised if his mother has previously lost two children through bleeding at the *brit;* and if two sisters each lose a son through bleeding at the *brit,* a boy born to a third sister may not be circumcised. The Talmud (Yevamot 64b) appears to suspect the transmission of hemophilia through the female line.

There are no comparable ceremonies to change a girl into a woman. Of course, the circumcision of the boy defines her place in society as it is defining his, but her name is given by her father, in the synagogue, among males. The girl receives no instruction in the laws or sacred languages, no education that would enable her to participate in the synagogue or question or interpret the "culture" she is learning.[5] She might learn to read the folk language—Yiddish (Hebrew-German), Judeo-Spanish or Ladino (Hebrew-Spanish), or one of the Judeo-Arabic languages—but her knowledge is transmitted through informal instruction, songs, and stories. She becomes adept at keeping the house and her ability to earn a living through a small business might free her father or brothers, or husband, for study.

At twelve and a day a girl may be betrothed; at twelve and a half, married. At this age, even if unmarried, she assumes her adult ritual duties except for lighting the candles. (That duty comes with marriage.) As was true of her brother, her social maturity is decreed, but whereas his transformation is related to his mastery of "culture's" laws, hers is linked to the onset of a natural function, menstruation. Unlike her brother, the girl is never separated from the home; she is given an education that teaches her how to care for children and to prepare the food. Even the responsibility for the laws most incumbent upon her, the laws of menstrual purity, is ultimately out of her hands because of her lack of formal instruction in the Law. Although, according to the Talmud, "Because of three transgressions women die in childbirth, because they are negligent in the observance of the periods of menstrual uncleanliness, in the separation of the dough portion, and in the lighting of the Sabbath candles" (Sabbath II, 6), the Code of Jewish Law states that it is the duty of the husband to instruct his wife in the laws of menstrual purity, its procedures, calculations, and self-examinations. Of course, women do transmit information, but all questions of practice ultimately must be referred to a male, the rabbi. The male's control of the Law gives him control over women even in those areas most affecting the woman herself. She is socially constrained and defined through her associations with the natural phenomena of childbirth, blood, fire and food. She is responsible for upholding the Law but locked out of the process of ordering it through definition, the study of the Torah, which produces control over the society. She stands between "nature" and

5. Although the woman is welcomed in the synagogue, her presence is minimized through her separation behind a partition, often in a gallery.

"culture," in a compromised, ambiguous position that makes her appear threatening in a culture that values strict categorical definition. "Woman," although a polar term, is inherently imprecise.

The Talmud acknowledges this imprecision in the definition of "woman" when it states that "a woman is a *golem* [a shapeless lump] who must marry only a man who can transform her into a [finished, useful] vessel, in accordance with the line from Isaiah (54:5): 'For thy Maker is thy husband' (Sanhedrin 22b)" (Feldman 1974:34).[6] The Talmud uses the metaphor in the Torah of the relationship of the society to God to explain the relationship of wife to husband. In Isaiah it is the society itself that is likened to clay in the hands of the potter (45:9); in the talmudic quotation, that which is less fixed and formed and subject to control is expressed through the image of the female.

This imprecision in the definition of "woman" mirrors the imprecision in the concept of the natural world, with which she is associated. Nature, as described up to now, is something people can control through mind and will, but Jewish society also recognizes a side of nature that has ultimate control over all mankind. "Nature" in Judaism is a double concept enveloping "culture," for it is both subordinate and superordinate to society's designs. It is the raw experience that can be managed, and it is the values and eternal truths that justify society's laws.

The concept of the female in Judaism has been used to connote both aspects of "nature." Whereas the man occupies himself with the rules of society, which appear to "mediate" between God and the people, the woman's role is to care for individuals and to work through direct, personal, "unmediated" relationships. Yet this commitment to individuals also implies grand, synthesizing concepts that transcend social categories: the inherent, unrationalized kinship relationship of the community, and, through the relationship of the woman to her husband, the relationship of the community to its Maker. The dual connotations of the symbol of the female in Judaism are described by Ortner in terms of more general reference:

> Mothers tend to be committed to their children as individuals, regardless of sex, age, beauty, clan affiliation, or other categories in which the child

6. The idea of a woman as one who must be formed and controlled is also found in the other meaning of the word *golem*. Although the first use of the word, in Psalm 139:16, is in the sense of an "unformed substance," the term came to mean also a stupid person, one who does not know what he does not know. In medieval legends incorporating kabbalistic ideas, a *golem* was a piece of clay that might come to life if the divine name were placed on its lips.

might participate. Now any relationship with this quality—not just mother and child but any sort of highly personal, relatively unmediated commitment—may be seen as a challenge to culture and society "from below," insofar as it represents the fragmentary potential of individual loyalties vis-à-vis the solidarity of the group. But it may also be seen as embodying the synthesizing agent for culture "from above," in that it represents generalized human values above and beyond loyalties to particular social categories. Every society must have social categories which transcend personal loyalties, but every society must also generate a sense of ultimate moral unity for all its members above and beyond those social categories. [1974:83]

The concepts that develop out of her particular activities are reinforced by the woman's association with undifferentiated physical substances used to suggest continuity and immediacy—water, fire, blood. The female is both a "shapeless lump" that must be controlled by the Law, and, paradoxically, a being whose relationship with the divine bypasses the Law. Woman's ambiguous status has taken many forms in daily life. She has been treated as both the source of good and as an evil temptress who can turn the man away from contemplation of the Law; she has been glorified, as in the recitation by the husband on the Sabbath extolling the "woman of valor" whose "price is above rubies," but, at the same time, she has been separated and tabooed during her menstrual periods. The symbolic underpinnings of the laws of menstrual purity, so crucial to the woman and the community, do not necessarily dictate a negative state for the woman at that time, but ideal forms do not stay ideal, and a practice may acquire a new meaning unless the whole symbolic matrix from which it is born is kept intact. Part of the problem in viewing the woman and her relationship to the purity of the community is that the natural property immediately involved, blood, like the woman, has come to suggest ambiguity as a result of, or despite, the society's attempt to enclose it in order.

Blood, expressive at once of life and death, is honored and tabooed at the same time. Blood may not be eaten: "Since the life of a living body is in its blood . . . no one among you, not even a resident alien, may eat blood" (Leviticus 17:11–12). As a powerful representation of the sacred, blood must be handled with extreme care, much as one handles the sacred Law. Blood spilled on the ground must be covered with earth, as worn out scrolls of the Torah must be buried.

Blood defies society's attempts to limit it by definition because, as a carrier of life, it appears inherently to participate in the realms of both God and man. As "life," blood suggests the eternal, God, and the soul after death, but the shedding of blood also signifies the temporal, and death. It is this power to compromise categorical limits that makes blood, like all ambiguous forms, dangerous to the system as a whole, and hence feared and subjected to rigid rules of contact.

In acknowledgment of its role as a carrier of life, blood is used as a medium of expression of the relationship between man and God. But first blood must be brought under the control of the rules that order society. In ancient times, the blood of sacrifice was used to dedicate new shrines, ordain priests, and mark the covenant. The ordination of Aaron and his sons was carried out by placing sacrificial blood on their right ears, hands, and feet, and by pouring the rest of the blood on all sides of the altar. The blood of all sacrifices was dashed on the altar; during Passover, the priests collected blood from all the individual sacrifices brought to the Temple and poured it at the base of the altar. Today, no circumcision is complete unless a drop of blood is drawn during daylight hours, thus marking the covenant. In the past, the circumciser would press his mouth, with wine in it, to the wound, to stop the bleeding. This semi-ecclesiastic could touch the blood with his mouth because blood from the body of a young child announcing the covenant connotes the highest purity.

Only blood controlled by human action in accordance with the Law can be permitted, and hence honored. Control in Judaism is used for moderation; excess in any form is curtailed. As the absence of the Law suggests chaos, so uncontrolled, excessive blood suggests wildness, disorder, lack of safety, and death. Hunting is purposeless, since it is forbidden to eat animals that have not been slaughtered and whose blood has not been drained according to ritual procedure. Spilled blood suggests the emptying of life; so blood spilled on the ground is buried like a dead body. In this sense, the monthly pouring out of blood from the woman is seen as death, and like death to be avoided, feared, and contained.[7]

The emptying of blood also presages a new period in which life can be created; it is both an end and a beginning, and so a fearful, transitional state. The awareness of death and rebirth present during menstruation is carried in the concepts of *tum'ah* and *toharah*. *Tum'ah* suggests moral or spiritual impurity, a potentially contaminating state,

7. Semen is also considered a natural life force, and rules prohibit its indiscriminate waste through onanism. But semen, as exclusively male, representative of life only, and absent from the actual birth process, does not carry the negative implications of blood.

ritual uncleanliness; *toharah,* or ritual cleanliness, is the state of repurification and rebirth. By itself, *tum'ah* suggests death, evil, and pollution, but when connected with *toharah* through rituals that erase the
impure state, it becomes just another stage in the life cycle.

Before the destruction of the Temple, anyone who acquired
tum'ah through contact with a corpse cleansed himself through prescribed ritual means, and a man who "wasted his seed" through seminal
emission would cleanse himself from his impure state in a ritual bath
before studying the Torah or praying. Ever since the loss of the Temple,
some men have continued the custom of simulating death and rebirth
by purifying themselves of the evil of sin, *tum'ah,* through immersion
in the bath before holidays, and most especially before Yom Kippur and
Passover. But strict laws concerning ritual immersion have persisted
only in relation to women, and so, as Rachel Adler points out in a
comment on her article on *tum'ah* and *toharah* (1973:126), women's
practices have become divorced from the general symbolism of death
and resurrection that related them to the rest of the culture.

The culture's emphasis after the dispersion on the need for moral
perfection in order to hasten redemption, which resulted in the hardening of ritual prescriptions in all areas of daily life, worked to emphasize
the negative pole of the women's ritual. In trying to contain pollution,
the culture also tightened the means through which it contained and
controlled women.

The danger apparent during all times of transition became magnified as the balance between the positive and negative connotations of
women's ritual immersion was upset. Woman alone is to immerse herself regularly and so cleanse herself of *tum'ah.* Segregation during the
time of menstruation and the days immediately following, the *niddah*
("separation") period, became not just *tum'ah* in preparation for rebirth, but a taboo adhering to a source of evil. The laws pertaining to
menstrual purity have become a thing apart, studied by men and taught
to women, a means through which men, in their control of the Law,
control women, or, in structuralist terminology, the means through
which the distance between "culture" and "nature" is widened.

The way in which control over the administration of the rules of
society has supported the dominance of men and enclosed women can
be seen through an examination of the menstrual regulations. They not
only define the woman, but, by creating the conditions through which
a new member can enter society, also define the Jew.

The laws of menstrual separation and purification are understood as commandments from God (Leviticus 15:19–24), and an entire tractate of the Talmud is devoted to discussion of these rules.[8] The injunction that a man must not lie with a woman during her "impure" time on pain of being cut off from the community is also found in Leviticus 18:19 and 20:18.

First there is the definition of time: the woman is "impure" for about two weeks, the time of the flow itself and for seven intermediary "white" days after. She then "purifies" herself in the prescribed manner at night by completely lowering herself into the ritual bath, allowing the water to touch every part of her body. The menstrual laws also pertain to the period after childbirth, the only difference being that instead of the seven-day "white" period after routine menstruation and after the birth of a boy, the woman must wait fourteen days after the birth of a daughter before immersing herself in the ritual bath.[9] The ritual nature of the immersion is emphasized by the thorough cleansing that precedes it. Although the original source of water for the ritual bath, or *mikveh* ("collection of waters"), must be natural, a natural stream or lake is not automatically suitable as a *mikveh*.[10] A *mikveh* requires rabbinical supervision, and in the view of the most orthodox, the use of a lake or stream needs the prior approval of a rabbi Through male rabbinical designation and supervision, a natural form— the rain water, the lake—becomes a product of "culture," and acts as a cultural agent in transforming that aspect of nature Jewish women share with all other women into a specifically Jewish state.[12]

This process of transformation is especially important in giving the child his initial identity as a Jew in terms of his mother. By making the process of reproduction "Jewish," the "natural" relation of mother and child is made "Jewish"; pure "nature" is "culturized" from the start, and the child is never the same, even before birth, as the child of a

8. Leviticus 15 also lists the rules governing purification after male emissions.

9. No reason for the additional seven days is given. Perhaps the birth of another potential carrier of blood appears doubly dangerous, and the protective power of the number seven (see chapter 6) is doubly invoked. Instead of seven days separating the fearsome blood and its message of intrusion of the sacred into the temporal dimension, twice seven are necessary. Of course, one could look at the other side of the coin and say that twice seven marks the birth of a daughter as especially fortunate.

10. Provision is made to collect rain water.

Hoenig (1969:48).

12. It should be noted that those branches of Judaism most concerned with the continuation of ritual structures, the Orthodox and the Conservative movements, are those that are still reluctant to allow women to enter the rabbinate.

gentile. By making each woman's reproductive state a matter of societal concern, the concepts of kin and community, "nature" and "culture," are merged.

The laws of *niddah* also serve to promote conception at the most opportune time in the life-bearing vessel, just after it has been purified. Since husband and wife have been separated for about two weeks, it is highly likely that intercourse will occur during the first few days after the wife returns from the *mikveh,* and, indeed, "it is the duty of every husband to visit his wife on the night she has performed the ritual of immersion" (Code of Jewish Law, vol. 4, 150:8). This time period corresponds with the time of greatest probable fertility. For a society that envisages itself as a "nation of priests" and is concerned with survival, the proper state of the means of perpetuating the community is of paramount importance.

Through the mother, the child receives his eternal, Jewish affiliation, which contrasts with the historical, tribal affiliation he will later get through his father. At birth, the child is a "natural" Jew, born in a vessel made sacred through the laws of menstrual purity administered by the society in fulfillment of the covenant. This activization of the covenant makes the conditions of birth not only sacred but particularly "Jewish." The blood present at birth is a reminder of the intrusion of God's power over life and death into the world of man, and the fact that this intrusion comes within limits set by God himself in Leviticus reinforces the concept of the unique covenantal relationship within which the child is born. "Jewishness" is an inherent attribute of the child born within the strict conditions of the Law; it is an identity, a classification, prior to any choice or action taken by the child or society.

Although the child is classified as a "Jew" because of the conditions of his birth, he does not yet have a place in the historical dimension of the society. This comes with the giving of his name, through which the eternal and temporal coordinates of the child's existence meet. The name connotes the presence of a particular, enduring soul, created, according to talmudic legend, at the beginning of the world.[13]

At the same time, the name delineates the child's historical antecedents by identifying each individual in relation to his or her father and

13. One of the daily morning prayers, taken from the Talmud, says: "My God, the soul which thou hast placed within me is pure. Thou hast created it; thou hast formed it; thou hast breathed it into me. Thou preservest it within me; thou wilt take it from me and restore it to me in the hereafter" (Berakhot 60b).

tribal forefathers through the male line.[14] To be a member of the society is to be placed in the sequence of time, to share in the community's past and in its destiny, and to begin the progression through the stages of bodily and social maturity. This placement in history can come only after the child's nature is consecrated through the conditions of birth.

The practical effect of giving the name in this way is that the child grows up cognizant of his or her relationship to the persons in the Torah, whether it be Moses and the rest of the Levites, the family of Aaron, the high priests, or members of the lay tribes, collectively called Israel. The historical figures are also the child's kin.

The different conditions under which a boy and a girl receive their names reinforce their future relationship to the group. The boy's name is given to him in person, in a ritual that necessarily includes him and marks him bodily and incorporates him not only into the society as a whole, but also into the more restricted segment that administers the rules. On the other hand, neither the girl nor her mother is present in the synagogue when her father gives her the name that links her to past generations. Her name is announced on the Sabbath following her birth (or on the other days the Torah is read publicly, Monday and Thursday), in the context of a special prayer wishing her health and happiness. So soon after the birth, the mother is still under the postchildbirth regulations prohibiting her entry into the synagogue. The female's connection with the divine is exhibited through the necessary "active" presence of the Torah at the time her name is first announced, but the fact that it is given by and through the company of males underscores the male's role as the agent of God in controlling the female.

Today more attention is paid to the naming of a girl among Jewish groups that permit female participation in synagogue ritual. The name may be given with the mother's name as well as the father's, at a time when the mother can be present, and with other rituals and readings added to give the ceremony an importance comparable to that of the *brit*. However, even if the name of the mother's tribe were given, the child's tribal identification would necessarily remain in the male line, since the mother's tribe is that of her father.

14. The association of the child with history through the male line is graphically emphasized in some congregations by having the actual circumcision take place on a board that comes out from the seat of the Chair of Elijah, which normally remains empty for the "presence" of the prophet. The godfather or "holder" *(sandek)* sits in the chair and spreads his legs, and the child is placed on the board between them. This is the custom in Curaçao, Netherlands Antilles.

This fact has importance at the time of the *Pidyon HaBen,* the Redemption of the First-born. At this time, the mother's lineage is considered even among traditionalists because a male child is not to be redeemed if his mother is of a priestly line. The priestly designation itself indicates both a historical and an ahistorical placement: the Levite caste and the hereditary line of Aaron the High Priest were created at a particular moment in time, after Sinai, but they also represent an eternal, intermediate relationship between God and the rest of the Jews or, when the Jews are seen collectively as the priestly people, between God and the rest of mankind. At the *Pidyon HaBen,* the only time when the mother's lineage is considered, it would appear that when the priestly identification is also carried by the bearer of the child's eternal identification as a Jew, the eternal aspects of the child's existence "outweigh" the historical, and the child cannot be redeemed. His identification as a priest is part of his eternal, natural identification as a Jew, and is not subject to any restructuring by society.

Within the society, the man acts through limit and word to reach God; woman's paths to God lie in undifferentiated means such as fire, water, and blood. The uncontrollable blood that makes her socially "impure" and limits her actions in relation to her husband does not interfere with her relation to God through the performance of her ritual duties in the home. Although she cannot touch her husband, or sit at a table with him unless an object is placed between them, the woman continues to light the candles and burn the portion of bread dough that dedicates each new loaf to God.

Together, man and woman act to fulfill the Law, but as long as control of that Law rests with him, she appears as a complementary, lesser or imperfect part of man, as Eve was created out of a part of Adam. In this sense, the woman's activities in the home provide a contrast that supports and allows the functioning of the male universe with the synagogue at its center. Each realm is completed through the actions of the other; together there is harmony. A second sense of the female, however, is implied in the first. She is a mediator, a facilitator, one through whom the good and evil in nature flow. She can contain evil by adhering to her duties and in the process invite blessings. She can invite disaster, and hinder the community's, and her husband's, quest for purity and goodness by ignoring her responsibilities. The man needs a pure wife to be complete: the order "be fruitful and multiply" is incumbent on the man, not the woman. It is his wife who "facilitates" this command, not for her own sake but for his, and for the whole society.

The power of the woman can be seen in a story from the Talmud illustrating the saying "woman determines man's behavior". A couple lived together for ten years. Having no children, they said to each other, "We are no profit to God," and so they were divorced. The man married an impious woman, and she transformed him into a man of wickedness. The woman married a man of wickedness, and she transformed him into a man of goodness (Trattner 1955:84). The Code of Jewish Law insists on the importance of a good wife, so much so that "it is mandatory to divorce a bad woman who is of a quarrelsome disposition and is not as modest as a respectable woman in Israel should be, even if it is the first marriage" (vol. 4, 145:24).

In mystical Judaism, the relations of male and female present in talmudic Judaism have been made part of a symbolic system that describes communal relations and Israel's relation to God in idealized familial terms. The interdependence of male and female is changed from the interplay of separate but complementary relations of "dominance" and "subordinance," or "culture" and "nature," to a matter of unification of the separated realms, as stated in sexual imagery. In mystical Judaism, the "Community of Israel" assumes female attributes, and through recognition of dependency and expressions of love calls out for its divine, "male" lover:

> So with the Community of Israel: whenever previously she was in exile, at the appointed time, she was wont of herself to return to the King; now, in this exile, the Holy One, be blessed, will go and take her by the hand and raise her, and give her comfort, and bring her back to his palace. [Scholem 1949:111]

Life on earth is seen as paralleling a cosmic drama of separation, love, and the yearning for union; the participants in the drama are always aware of, needing, and longing for each other. The symbols surrounding the man and woman reinforce this relationship while at the same time declaring the sexes distinct.

The images of mystical Judaism were widely accepted in eastern Europe, even by those not intimately familiar with the writings themselves, because through these images experience on earth gained coherence. Even now, they continue to influence Jewish thought. As with any art form, the Zohar and related works hold up quintessential ideas and emotions for observation and reflection. Works of art that are accepted by the society locate and allow contemplation of the preoccupations of their audience. By using the language of the most intimate of male-female relationships to express God's relation to Israel, the Zohar makes the divine relationship appear natural, and the biological one sacred.

In the Zohar, the woman as "facilitator" of man's commandments is not a passive instrument; although she is the medium through which man can have children, the order to multiply is applied to the female also. In the words of the Zohar, the woman must be as a cultivated field, ready and alluring, which will stimulate the life-giving rain from above. This "lower world"—the woman, the Community of Israel, the Israel-ites in Egypt—must call out to the "upper world"—the man and God —if sacred union is to take place.

Both aspects of the female are intertwined in the concept of the Shekinah, the indescribably beautiful, ideal feminine "part" of God. The idea of the Shekinah in talmudic Judaism indicates only the pres-ence of God in the daily affairs of the people, but in the Kabbala the Shekinah was given more specific female identity, not as God's oppo-site, but as an intrinsic aspect of God that has been torn away and still yearns for reconciliation.

In mystical thought, all creation proceeded from, and will return to, the unity of God. Dualism does not exist; strained separation does. The feminine Shekinah, exiled from her greater part and wandering the earth, came to represent the situation of the Jews, separated and aching for their god and their land. Whether or not the mystical story of Creation involving the sundering of the male-female aspects of God was accepted or even known, this image of God's reachable "Dwell-ing," "Presence," or "Light" that follows the Jews in their exile was adopted in many eastern European communities. During the Middle Ages, men would wander from town to town in eastern Europe as mendicants and mourners in order to share the "exile of the Shekinah." Through penance they hoped to hasten the end of the estrangement of the Shekinah, and of Israel, and God. This divine tension has also been used to express the relationship of husband and wife.

The Shekinah is said to be present in the perpetual light on the eastern wall of the synagogue and in candlelight in general. It shines through the hands of the priestly *kohen* delivering a blessing, on ten men praying, on the chaste, on the benevolent, and on a husband and wife living together in harmony. Men may experience the Shekinah as the "bride" or "queen" of the day of unity, the Sabbath, and through the Torah, a pure soul, or a righteous woman. It is because of a good wife that the Shekinah enters the home, and it is because of a good wife that she accompanies the man in his wanderings from home.

The Talmud identifies the Shekinah with the moon: "Whoever pronounces the benediction over the new moon in its due time welcomes, as it were, the presence of the Shekinah" (Sanhedrin 42a). In the Zohar, the woman is represented by the moon, whose only light is a reflection from the "male" sun, but a full moon is synonymous with the wisdom of the heart—the wisdom of the feminine:

> Kabbalistically speaking, the moon (Shekinah) of the dream world, which is feminine in itself, wanes or withdraws its light from man when he sins. The dream world is a sphere of feminine activity through which wisdom may be attained. This attainment of wisdom is symbolized by the full moon, the feminine principle, without which the Kabbalists insist man is incomplete. . . . His wisdom is the wisdom of the feminine—or the heart, and not just of the mind or intellect. [Ponce 1973:273–74]

For the Jews in exile, the Shekinah-God symbol has many facets. As the longed-for reunion between *Kehillat Israel* (the Community of Israel) and God would come to pass on both ideal and physical planes, so the imagery expressing the relationship between the earthly Israel and her divine lover is romantic and frankly sexual. The lyrical Song of Songs of Solomon, which is customarily read at the conclusion of the Seder and often on the Sabbath, is interpreted in this light.

> By night on my bed I sought him whom my soul loveth;
> I sought him, but I found him not.
> 'I will rise now, and go about the city,
> In the streets and in the broad ways,
> I will seek him whom my soul loveth.'
> I sought him, but I found him not.
> The watchmen that go about the city found me:
> 'Saw ye him whom my soul loveth?'
> Scarce had I passed from them,
> When I found him whom my soul loveth:
> I held him, and would not let him go.
> Until I had brought him into my mother's house,
> And into the chamber of her that conceived me. [3:1–4]

The Shekinah has other faces. She is the supernal mother, begging the supernal king for mercy for her children on the Day of Atonement, and acting through unqualified love just as Rachel, in the Book of Jeremiah, weeps for her lost children in exile. She is the Virgin of Israel, whose total purity is stressed on the day of purity, the Sabbath. But these ideal images of the Shekinah were never divorced from the image of female lover, and they represent multiple aspects of the female present in the male-female relationship. As the Shekinah represents reunion on both the ideal plane and, as the return to the Land, on the physical one, so her ideal, ethereal qualities of absolute love, mercy, and purity are expressed through a metaphor for the most physical of activities.[15]

The Shekinah provides an image for the ideal social relationship as well as a language for a man's relationship to God. As divine unity presupposes the merging of the male and female "aspects" of God, so a man must be in a "male-female" state at all times. On a practical level, this means that a man is incomplete without a wife, just as a woman needs a man to make her "whole." On a more ideal level, the desired female is the Shekinah, not the carnal woman. Man reaches God first through merging with the Shekinah, whom he meets in the Torah,[16] through the Sabbath, and through his wife. Carnal love is acceptable and good, especially on the Sabbath; in fact, the Shekinah is said to rejoice when physical union parallels divine unity on this day of holy unity. And, after a trip, a man must pleasure his wife, for it is because of her that God's presence is in his home.

Conversely, of course, an unrighteous woman closes her home to the Shekinah, denies her husband the Shekinah's companionship when away, and may tempt him into bodily passions unmediated by the mind. Although the male is conceived of as the active, dominant partner in the relationship, the female's role is not passive. By adhering to culture's rules and by socializing the young, she enables the culture's promises to be fulfilled; if she misuses her potential, she destroys them.

Through the symbol of the ideal feminine, man's paths to the divine—the synagogue and the home—are united, and "the nature of culture" in Judaism is itself made problematic. More and more, "culture" appears as "a small clearing in the forest of the larger, natural system" (Ortner 1974:85). In implementing the categories and rules that

15. Despite their apparent similarity, the Shekinah and the Virgin Mary are not the same. Mary, the ideal mother, is never a carnal being; the Shekinah, like an earthly mother, "enjoys" carnal love. Mary has achieved an independent form through picture and statue; the ban on iconography in Judaism has served to prevent such an independent status and preserve the Shekinah as a projection of God, an ideal "Adam's rib." Mary is understood as a historical being; the Shekinah is an ahistorical emanation that has intruded into history and will return to God when redemption comes.

16. The man who completes the last portion of the Torah in the yearly cycle is called the Bridegroom of the Torah, and the one who starts the cycle immediately afterwards is called the Bridegroom of Genesis *(Hatan Bereshit).* The act of removing the ornate, jeweled wrappers of the Torah in preparation for reading is an honor called "disrobing the Torah."

define a community as separate from and superior to nature and other societies, "culture" appears dominant. Yet, in Jewish thought these laws have never been understood merely as human creations, and the man studies the Torah to comprehend the eternal mind behind it. Hasidic writings warn against being fooled by the "garments of the Torah," its narrations, laws, and words, and compares them to the outer layers of an onion that must be peeled away to reach the inner, hidden core.

The attempt, particularly in mystical Judaism, to comprehend this inner reality is a "culture"-to-nature process.[17] "Culture" is limitation and codification; nature is pure potential, understood in Judaism as the omniscient, omnipotent God. The Torah, as laws for society, is "culture;" but as revelation, it is a means to reach beyond man's finite capacities to a boundless world. The concept of revelation also makes "culture" part of nature; the laws are understood as expressions of reality itself, principles of social action consistent with the functioning of a universe that is eternal and impervious to human domination.[18]

Female imagery is used to express the range of possibilities of the natural world, from uncontrolled animality and death to the highest forms of life in beauty, eternity, mercy, and divine harmony. It is in the home that all these possibilities meet, and it is at the Seder, in particular, that all these diverse concepts—woman and man, home and synagogue, kin and community, God and society—come together in meaningful form. As a structured teaching event whose text recounts the Exodus theme ever-present in the liturgy, the Seder might seem to belong in the synagogue. But the Seder, like the woman, is "compromised culture." Despite its text and order, the ritual aims at the extended community found only in the home, and not the more select congregation of adult males found in the synagogue. However, until recent innovations in education for women and more liberal translation of the Haggadah, the text remained in the hands of the men. Written in Hebrew, the Haggadah has been inaccessible to most women and girls except as translated by the men. And yet the language has never been a barrier to communication of the Seder's messages because the ritual includes many other media through which the story may be transmitted. The gathering in the home of family and friends, the sensi-

17. Chapter 19 of *Likutei Amarim* by Rabbi Schneur Zalman of Liadi, one of the founders of Hasidism, identifies the inaudible world lying beyond the audible world with nature: "Nature is a loan word for anything that is not in the realm of reason or comprehension." (1972:113)

18. Of course, it might be objected that this view of nature is itself a product of "culture." This is the perspective from without.

ble forms of matzah, wine, and bitter herbs, the candlelight and songs, all contribute to the meanings being constructed through the recitation of the Haggadah.

As a more or less balanced state between formal and informal transmission of "culture," the Seder combines male and female ways of teaching. The Seder's formal structure is constantly being challenged by a song that runs too long, a sleepy or restless child, laughing and joking by those who are enjoying the wine, or questions about history and custom. The order and the rules regulate the transmission of some of the most important ideas of the culture, and so administration of the Seder resides with those in charge of "culture," the men. But the conditions of transmission are closer to a female activity, the teaching in the home of those who may be nonliterate and restless. The wine makes even the adults more relaxed and informal than they are in the synagogue. As a ritual mandated by God each year, the ceremonial telling of the Exodus story is more important than any specific form it may take. Therefore, despite the customary leadership of the male, a woman may act as leader if no adult male is present, and the home setting and conditions of transmission support her activity.

The merging of the concepts of family and community through the home is reinforced by the performance of two Seders among more traditional groups, instead of the one Passover observance mandated by the Torah. The doubling of the first day of the festival and the Seder has had the effect of doubling the size of the community with which one shares the ritual. Often different guests, different members of the extended family, are invited each night.

In a very concrete way, the Seder has been used to express the convergence of the separated personal, social, and ritual spheres of female and male. On their wedding day, the bride's gift to her new husband has often been a prayer shawl and a Haggadah.

5
The Created Society

A chicken is not born kosher.
Advertisement for
frozen poultry

The Seder celebrates the creation of culture itself, and of the Jews as the carriers of its highest form, by its handling of the items and persons present at the ritual.

As discussed before, "culture" implies domination through discrimination, and, in the process, the creation of something new. Discernment is the conscious value of Jewish culture that is implicit in all actions. The Talmud states it this way: "Where there is no Torah there is no culture; and where there is no culture there is no Torah. . . . Where there is no knowledge there is no discernment, and where there is no discernment there is no knowledge" (Sayings of the Fathers, 3:21). In the Torah, Adam's first act as a being created in the image of God is one of domination through discernment. In Genesis, naming connotes domination: God names man (1:10; 2:7), and man names woman (2:23) and each of the animal species (2:19–20).

There are levels of discrimination that can be made, and are made, in Jewish thought. The primary stage of "culture" is the perception of differences and the assigning of names to them. At this level the world is divided into sexes, species, social groups. The criteria for the divisions vary with those constructing them, but the result of this process of ordering is a kind of freedom for man: once categories are established, nature assumes a predictable, manageable form. Even wild masses of wind and water can be separated into "hurricanes," then given "personal names" like David or Agnes, and "tracked." Man can act as if he has control over matter and as if undifferentiated matter, continuum, chaos itself, did not exist. If there are threats to his order, they can be managed. Items can be redefined and transformed, and even ambiguity can be contained through the imposition of ritual form.

But a further, secondary process of selection also occurs. Once the basic distinctions between social groups or natural phenomena are made, the society continues to refine only those distinctions that express its own ethos or perspective. The term "foreigners" subsumes and blends diverse peoples and modes of action, while the word "Frenchman" or "Russian" receives more minute definition, and "barbarians" are all those without the code of conduct of the society affixing the label. "Israel" and "Jew" express through the idea of a covenant a primary distinction from all "gentiles," but the meanings of "Jew" and "Israel" have been highly developed as contrasted with "gentile," which remains an internally undifferentiated term.

Especially where Jews have lived in cohesive communities, the focus of Jewish thought has been inward, on all the permutations of thought and action possible in the Torah, while seeing the outside world as a more or less monolithic bloc. Like social groups, forms of natural life that have a potential as food have been divided for all time into those that are inside the walls of the Torah and those that are not. Despite anyone else's perception of the shrimp, it is not recognizable as "food" in Judaism. Although shellfish is distinguished, named, and categorized, Jewish interest in it is only for the purpose of ensuring that it is kept out of the society. By contrast, the rules governing the care and processing of those animal forms permitted "inside" are highly elaborated. To be permitted as a possible food does not guarantee that the animal may be eaten; from birth to the table the animal is examined for imperfection, cared for in a particular manner when alive, and then slaughtered, cleaned, cooked, and eaten according to prescription.

Although all of nature is "tamed" when brought under man's mental control, Judaism has further domesticated a part of nature by bringing it under the same Law that structures the life of each Jew. As will be seen in detail later in this chapter, through the Law, man, animal, and vegetable become homologous, and each becomes a means for realizing the Law in daily life. "Culture," then, must be understood on two levels, as mankind's universal ability to impose order on the world of experience, and then as the specific way in which this human necessity to order is manifested in a society.

Lévi-Strauss sees the process of differentiation as the foundation of society. When in Judaism the laws as a means of differentiation are seen as proceeding from divine and not human nature, the resultant culture is raised above all others as divine process. The highly refined laws of Judaism that have bounded Jewish society have simultaneously served to increase its internal value. Because every decision implies a value judgment, as objects, actions, and ideas are excluded, the inside world is enhanced.

The Seder celebrates the creation of a culture by exhibiting "culture" in its most pristine form. Each item and each person at the table is a "cultural" product: as each goblet and each plate must be in a state of perfection, so each person and each food must be as perfectly as possible in accord with the laws of "culture." This perfection is reflected in new clothes and in the extreme ritual cleanliness of the home with its new paint and new shelf paper.

The weeks of preparation for the festival intensify this awareness of a universe perfected according to the Law. In the Jewish world, the distinction between sacred and profane is a daily matter; the profane is not a period of time but a state of alienation from, or disobedience to, the Law. The transition from ordinary time to the special time of the great festival is accomplished through increased attention to a rigorous set of holiday rules that focus the mind and demand acquiescence to the Law. As children help mother and grandmother ritually and nonritually clean the house, change to the holiday dishes, and prepare special foods, they experience the Law as a matter-of-fact imperative. Each year in America there are questions about the acceptability of new food products as Passover items. The answers are sometimes disputed, but even the disputation implies a reference to an absolute standard.

While the woman perfects the home, the man prepares himself by attending the special "Great Sabbath" services the week before Passover, and by immersing himself in the ritual bath. After weeks of hectic preparation, the Seder comes as both climax and relaxation, a state of heightened awareness and of willingness to accept the evening's ordering and the meanings carried by the unusual actions and foods.

The wine and bread of every festive meal assume a special form and role at the Passover ritual. Throughout the year wine and bread act as magnets for a range of thoughts inherent in the culture; this evening their altered state and their participation in a dialectical play of movement and sensation articulate the ideas and relationships within the society with even more clarity.

Wine and matzah represent the polarities of the culture in all their complexity: the society's preoccupation with moving all social forms toward a state of perfection as defined by the Law is dramatized by the continual opposition of these two foods. Exactly what the wine and matzah mean will become more comprehensible through an examina-tion of the processes of transformation—fire, water, blood, time, words —as they operate on all life forms at the Seder.

As they appear at the ritual table, animal, vegetable, and human life are in the form most expressive of "culture's" transformation of the raw materials of social experience. "Nature" as used here will describe those forms of life that are permitted within Jewish society to exhibit their raw, untransformed state. Of course, the very fact that they are permitted makes them products of discrimination and so "cultural," but the con-cern here is with the relation of the polarities and the transformation that operates within a society. Here "nature" and "culture" point to the ideals to which items must conform in accordance with Jewish law.

According to the Torah, meat may be eaten only from mammals that chew the cud and have split hooves, and from birds not specifically prohibited. No bird that acts as a scavenger may be eaten. "Swarming things," whether insects, moles, mice, lizards, or crocodiles, may not be eaten, nor may any form of life found in the water that lacks fins and scales (Leviticus 11; Deuteronomy 14). Anatomical distinctions are used to mark the "clean" from the "unclean," but they are not the cause of the "uncleanliness." "Uncleanliness" is the result of being placed out-side the Law. In addition, even permitted forms are prohibited if their death occurs from other than ritual means. If the death is not due to an action of the culture, if death is not "tamed," then the animal assumes the same outside, wild status as other prohibited creatures such as the vulture or the raven.

Meat for the table, then, can come only from animals made "in-side," and so mentally or actually domesticated. Such animals share the same rules of society as the Jew and are considered to be included in the covenant. Cattle must also rest on the Sabbath, and first-born male animals, as well as first-born male children, are dedicated to God's service. The permitted animal must be slaughtered with one, swift, clean stroke of the knife by a ritual slaughterer, severing the jugular vein, windpipe, and gullet and so causing a gush of blood, anemia to the brain, and instant unconsciousness. The vital organs are then examined to ensure that the animal is free from any defect that might have caused its death had it not been slaughtered. Only the forequarters of the animal may be used as food.

Before eating, meat must be further prepared by soaking and salt-ing. This process removes the most identifiable mark of the live animal, its blood, and yields a "cultural" product for the table. Both water and salt have purifying, transforming roles in Jewish culture. Ritual hand-washing precedes every meal, and ritual immersion separates the impure and pure states of the female, and transforms the gentile to Jew during conversion. On the afternoon of Rosh Hashana, the Jew may walk to the edge of a stream to ritually "throw his sins" into the amorphous water (*Tashlikh*, "thou wilt cast"). The white salt, which serves the immediate function of drawing out the blood, recalls the practice of salting the animal sacrificed at the Temple. Salt stood on the north side of the altar, and the preservative became the conscious symbol of the covenant between God and priest. Since the destruction of the Temple, salt has continued to be placed on each altar-in-exile: each dinner table is to have its salt cellar, and at each meal, bread must be salted before it is eaten. The Talmud states that a meal without salt is no meal (Berakhot 44a). Salt, as a reminder of the covenant, was also popularly understood as a ward against demons. The loud crackling of the fire might mean that one's enemies are plotting mischief, and the best way to frustrate such efforts is to throw salt into the fire. Salt thrown over the heads of the bride and groom is thought to protect them against demons jealous of the happiness of the wedding couple. The sacred and protective function of salt is seen in the custom among eastern European Jews of bringing salt and bread to a new home, as expressions of God's protection and sustenance.

Before meat reaches the table, its raw state is usually erased through cooking. Cooking brings the meat in contact with fire, and further alters its taste, texture, and appearance. This last transformation produces an object even more distanced from its natural state, and seals its identity as a "cultural" item.[1]

TABLE 1

The creation of food from animal life.

Nature
(permitted)
animal life
	Transformer
	blood, words, ritual
	    slaughtering;
	    salt and water;
	    cooking: fire
		Culture
		"food"

1. Poultry has its own conditions of edibility. Any injury to the bird renders it *trefah*. Feathers must be plucked in cold water; warm water would begin the cooking process while blood still remains.

Like the animal, the male is first given "inside" definition, transformed through specific acts, and then "cooked"—further transformed —through education and contact with a medium of conversion.

The male's transformation starts with the *brit*, which changes the natural child born to a Jewish mother into a "cultural" being and enters him on the process of becoming a responsible Jew that culminates with his first public Torah reading. At the *brit*, a cut is made, blood is drawn, and Hebrew words are said by the man officiating, the *mohel*, who, like the official at the ritual slaughtering, the *shohet*, is a semi-ecclesiastic. At this stage, the child is "in preparation" for adult status: this stage will be reached through education, that is, through increasing awareness of the Law and traditions, and therefore through the awakening of responsibility for self-perfection.

The child, as one who does not yet know enough, cannot be responsible for his ritual performance. The Seder, as an introduction to the culture's beliefs, is a stage in the transformation of the child. The child starts out pure, but through education ends in an indeterminate state, since awareness of the laws leaves him open to disobedience and hence possible sin. His life will be a struggle to know and enact the good, but he can never hope to achieve a state of absolute purity again. Conversely, meat begins in an indeterminate state, permitted but not perfected, and undergoes repeated transformations that result in its final state as a perfected cultural product.

The boy's final conversion is analogous to contact with fire. At his first public reading of the Law he comes publicly into contact with the immediacy of God, as the Israelites did at Sinai. His *Bar Mitzvah* ceremony is a demonstration of his ability to understand God's word and so to enter into communication with him. As at Sinai, the boy's conversion into an adult comes through the transformatory power inherent in Hebrew as a powerful intrusion of the divine into the world of man. The sacred language, *lashon hakodesh*, is the instrument of creation in Genesis, as well as the means of transformation at Sinai.[2] Hebrew benedictions introduce every meal and festival, marking the transition to a more sacred period, and they accompany physical communications with God such as candle lighting and ritual bathing.

"Cooking" is "domestication," a process that culminates in a final negation of the natural state and the creation of an object conforming to an ideational world. The female is never totally "cooked" since she

2. Some Orthodox today do not accept conversions or marriages performed by the liberal Reform wing of Judaism; they argue that Reform Jews do not believe in the concept of divine revelation at Sinai, and so in the possibility of actual transformation.

is barred from the disciplined study and responsibility for knowing and interpreting the Law which is the hallmark of the man's cultural state. No "cultural" mark is made on her person; her natural state can be defined but not absolutely controlled by the Law.

TABLE 2.

The social creation of the Jewish man.

Nature	Transformer	Culture
uncircumcised (Jewish) boy	blood, words, ritual cutting and removal of the natural part	adult male
	cooking: educational process, Hebrew, Torah	

A similar transformation takes place in the agricultural world. According to Leviticus (19:23–25), a fruit tree cannot be picked in the first three years. During that time it is called *orlah,* or uncircumcised, with the added connotations of "foreskin," "uncleanliness," and "insensibility." In the fourth year the fruit is to be dedicated to God. When the Temple was standing, fruit was brought as an offering; later, it became the custom to "redeem" the fourth-year fruit with a coin to charity, and then, before eating, to say the *Sheheheyanu* prayer (thanking God for having been permitted to reach that day) and benedictions over the fruit. Although today outside of Israel fourth-year fruits are not redeemed, grapes for wine still are, if cultivated by Jews. New grain *(hadash)* was forbidden until the second day of Passover, when a portion was offered in the Temple in celebration of the grain harvest.

TABLE 3.

The creation of "food" from agricultural products.

Nature	Transformer	Culture
(uncircumcised) fruit	time, offering (at Temple or charity), words	edible fruit
grain	time, offering, words	edible grain

Wine, like the woman, presents a special problem in "cultural" realization, since by its very nature it eludes containment in a fixed "cultural" state. And yet wine is a man-made product. Man can control its manufacture and definition, but not its inherent property of continual self-transformation through fermentation. All fruits and vegetables are unstable and go through cycles of birth, growth and decay. Their very composition makes them resistant to the state of fixed and ordered definition that "culture" implies. At all times, the rules governing the making of wine to be consumed by Jews are extremely stringent. Wine must be made only by Jews, and the conditions under which it may be handled by gentiles, even in closed bottles, are explicitly described (Cohen 1970:128). At Passover, the necessity of eliminating all contact with *hometz* means an alteration in the standard method of preparation. During the year, a wine yeast is added to the fruit to induce fermentation, but this yeast is considered *hometz* and is prohibited for Passover. Instead of adding yeast to the liquid, the juice of the grapes is exposed to air until it produces its own yeast; society's interference in the process is minimized, and one waits for the natural process to assert itself. Because of this requirement, the preparation of wine for the holiday necessarily anticipates its observance by many months.

TABLE 4.

Making wine Jewish.

Nature	*Transformer*	*Culture*
grapes from "redeemed" vines; naturally fermenting liquid	control by Jews; ordinary time: addition of yeast	"Jewish" wine
	Passover: segregation from leaven, long period of attention	Passover wine

At the Seder, sweet wine suggests joy and life, continuing at this festival its associations throughout the year. Wine is present on all occasions where future happiness is anticipated, such as the Sabbath, weddings, and the circumcision, and the common, informal toast over wine is *"L'chayim"*—"to life." It may be that wine is compatible with life and joy because of its sweet taste and its ability to suggest warmth and light, but these physical sensations are contingent and not necessary to its use. Other objects could be made to carry the same meanings. Wine is made "happy" by circumscribing its use. It is through mandated participation in situations defined as joyous that wine is a positive item, and through proscription in situations defined as sad—funerals or the days of mourning for the Temple—that wine becomes incompatible with the expression of individual or social despair. Although sweet wine is preferred at the Seder, a nonalcoholic fruit beverage may be substituted and, in context, provoke the same meanings.[3]

The drinking of wine is defined as a social event and is subject to the same rules of moderation that govern daily life in general. In Judaism, excess in any form is discouraged: "One should neither be too jocular and gay, nor too morose and melancholy; but should strive at all times to be happy, contented and friendly. And so with regard to other attributes a person who adopts the middle course is called wise" (Code of Jewish Law, vol. 1, 29:2). One is not to be celibate or engage in wanton sexual activity, nor is one to be so zealous in his study of the Torah that one neglects family obligations. The only exception to the rule of moderation is at Purim, when inebriation is permitted in celebration of the Jews' victory over tyranny in ancient Persia. Even at this time, however, this "excessive drinking" is in a context structured and circumscribed by the culture. There is a somewhat similar situation at the Seder.

Wine is drunk throughout the eight days of Passover and more wine is consumed at the Seder than at any other ritual. However, in prescribing the number of cups of wine, the Seder limits the excess and uses the changing physical state of the participants for its own ends of resolidifying communal bonds. Wine, so intimately connected in Jewish culture with social gatherings, connotes the erasing of the limits of the individual and the extension of himself to others. After making the Sabbath *Kiddush* benediction, the father sips the wine and passes it to his wife and children; at the *Havdalah* ceremony at the end of Sabbath, the men may sip from the common cup; and the bride and groom share the same wine. The infant at the *brit* demonstrates his incorporation into the society by sucking the wine placed on his lips (this wine is usually described as a sedative); later the adults drink together. At the Seder, the child "old enough to understand" must drink the wine, and the cup of wine standing ready for Elijah invites the prophet to become one with the community, and, in so doing, reinforce the intimate relationship between man and God. As the participants drink more and more wine, they relax the differences of status, wealth, and sex that divide them during the year. By drinking the liquor of life, they experience "community" as a hopeful, happy state.

As an amorphous form, wine—like water, blood, clouds, and smoke

3. Young children are often given grape juice or another fruit juice instead of wine.

—is used in Judaism to suggest "interconnectedness" between man and man, and man and God. Wine is considered incapable of absolute division; it retains its connected state even if poured into separate glasses. Therefore, wine can be the medium of social communion within the society, but cannot be used across societal boundaries. The very observant Jew cannot pour wine from his beaker into the glass of a non-Jew, but must serve him from a separate flask. Unlike kosher meat, which may be shared with gentiles if all other conditions for the meal are in accordance with the Law, the limits to which wine may be shared correspond to the limits of the community.

Wine, then, is the expression of sweetness, joy, communal bonds, and the individual's social life. Its presence on the Seder table awakens memories of happy, shared times. It also suggests impermanence, the flow of time, by its nature as an endlessly changing, decaying product, as well as by its association with rituals that mark changes in the life of a person. At the Seder, the wine exists in a dialectical relationship with the matzah. Whenever the wine cups are raised, the matzah is covered; whenever the bread is raised, the wine cups are empty. The common explanation for the covering of the matzah is that bread, as the most important food at any meal, would be insulted if it were to "see" the wine being so honored. In deference to its feelings, the bread is covered. This personalization of the bread is itself interesting, since other foods are not spoken of and treated so deferentially, and it contributes to an understanding of the language the matzah "speaks" as it "talks" with the wine at the Seder. In ordinary times, bread carries many meanings, and the form that bread takes at the Seder is, like the form of the Passover wine, very carefully planned to evoke concepts general to the culture and specific to the Seder. Before it can be ascertained just what role matzah takes in relation to wine, it is necessary to understand just what "bread" and "matzah" are.

During the rest of the year, bread is defined as dough that includes water, milk, wine, or oil, which act as agents of fermentation. Batters made solely with eggs or fruit juices fall into the category of "cake," which does not require the ritual handwashing and benedictions that precede the consumption of bread.[4] Bread is prepared by women, whose task it is to dedicate each new loaf to God by burning a small portion of the dough (or the heel of a loaf of bought bread), the *hallah*. (Cake dough is not burned.) This practice recalls the custom of giving

4. "Cake" therefore may be packed to eat on journeys where facilities for handwashing might be lacking.

a portion of each loaf of bread to the priest. The fire consumes and receives the *hallah* portion, purifying it and, by extension, the loaf, and allowing it to represent all the food on the table.

As in Exodus, when the Israelites of the desert are dependent on God for his gift of manna each day, bread is identified with sustenance itself, the gift of God. Eating becomes a "meal" and a ritual when bread is present; hallowed and dipped in the salt of the covenant, bread changes consumption to communion. On the day of the covenant, the Sabbath, a double portion of bread is present on the table, attesting to the intensified relationship of the day. This doubling is explained as recalling the double portion of manna that fell in the desert before the Sabbath. When the Temple was standing, each Sabbath the High Priest placed loaves of bread for display on the altar, in accordance with Leviticus 24:8: "He shall arrange them before the Lord regularly every Sabbath day—it is a commandment for all time on the part of the Israelites."

TABLE 5.

The creation of leavened bread.

Nature	*Transformer*	*Culture*
flour and water, leavening	fire, words	leavened bread

The prohibition of any leavened product is fundamental to the dietary laws of Passover. The customary requisite for a meal cannot be eaten in its usual form; leavened bread is replaced by the key symbol of Passover, the matzah. This replacement parallels the shift to a more sanctified time and a change in the perception of the table: the lesser altar outside Jerusalem becomes the High Altar of the Temple. Bread, as a product dedicated to God through fire, receives further cultural definition through the intricate rules governing its manufacture and use, rules that not only make it conform to a higher standard of purity but prepare it to serve as a focal point for the meanings of the Seder.

Matzah is made from flour that is guarded from the moment of milling to prevent contact with water and possible fermentation. The even purer matzah, the round *shmurah* ("guarded") matzah preferred for the Seder, is prepared from flour watched from the time of harvesting. Some sources insist that *shmurah* matzah must be made by pious males; others say that only adults, male or female, may bake it. In communities in eastern Europe, non-*shmurah* matzah baking was usually a communal affair employing women and children and providing the poor with an annual source of extra income, but the man of the household was always responsible for the purity, through adherence to the rules of manufacture, of the matzah used in his home.

Matzah is baked quickly, taking no more than eighteen minutes from beginning to end, in a room shielded from the sunlight. Counters and rollers are sanded smooth to prevent the dough from being contaminated by a piece of dough from an earlier baking. The dough is rolled and pricked continuously to prevent rising. The water used must be cool and is preferably drawn from a well, at twilight the evening before, to stand through the night. The water cannot be used before daylight, but no rays of the sun may fall on it. No salt may be added to the matzah. The fire to bake the matzah ideally is started with willow branches saved from the Feast of Tabernacles, Sukkot, the fall before.

The cool, shielded water, drawn from the ground, which stands through the night and which retards fermentation, incorporates the ideas of death and God's distance into the baking process, but these ideas are balanced by the warmth of the fire and by the insistence on eighteen minutes as the time of complete preparation. Eighteen minutes is prescribed because fermentation is believed to start after this time. However, eighteen has other associations in Jewish thought. In Hebrew the letters for "18" also signify "life"; thus charitable donations are often made in multiples of eighteen, and many persons today wear the symbol for "18," *chai,* as a charm. The Sabbath candles, bringing God's light into the home, are kindled eighteen minutes before sundown. The baking process, like the Exodus, begins in the night and is completed in the daylight. In addition, the transitional season and experience of Passover is linked to the transitional season and experience of early fall through the fire started with the branches from Sukkot. Sukkot commemorates the period of wandering in the desert after the Exodus, and the willows especially convey the sense of precariousness that is part of the Passover Festival of Liberation. The willows get their name from the synagogue procession in which they are carried: *Hoshana,* or "Save, I pray Thee."

It is the men, the interpreters of the Law, who take over the baking of the matzah, either by doing it themselves or by overseeing its production. This contrasts with the woman's responsibility for the changeable leavened bread. Like the woman, the fruit, and the wine, leavened bread becomes "culture" through word and action but cannot assume a fixed state due to inherent properties. Although all forms of life, including the human body, will someday decay, the essence of the "cultural" in Judaism is the selection from among these forms of those that best represent decay's antithesis.[5]

Like meat and men, the matzah reaches a state congruent with "culture" in its highest form.

TABLE 6.

The creation of matzah.

Nature	Transformer	Culture
flour and water	rules of manufacture, control by males	matzah

The result of the baking process is a product that, in sensible form, is the opposite of wine. Where wine is wet, colorful, tasty, "hot," and unstable, unleavened bread is dry, white, bland, cool, and lasting. As created by the rules—in contrast with the hurried baking in Exodus—unleavened bread becomes distinct both from the form of bread widely used by modern desert peoples and from the flat wafers of the Catholic communion. It becomes "matzah," a unique cultural form suited to the constructs of the society. It is not just "desert bread," but bread of the specific desert of Sinai—and of the *galut*.

The desert in Exodus is more than a physical location. As a world without change, except as decreed by God, it is nature presented in a form most analogous to Judaism's idea of culture, the realization of God's eternal laws.

The wilderness of the Exodus is nature lacking such sensual attributes as taste, smell, or color, and any forms that sustain life, unless they are provided by God. Where there is water, it is bitter, and there is no vegetation to feed either animals or people. God sends manna and dew in the morning, and quail in the evening, so that the Jews will not starve. The wanderers repeatedly curse God for bringing them to a place without water. God's control of water—the principal instrument of change in the natural world as well as the principal necessity for life—is underscored by the Israelites' numerous entreaties to God for water; by the brook that comes down from Mount Sinai and dissolves the remains of the golden calf (Deuteronomy 9:21); in the promises that if the Jews follow his commands God will provide the rain for their crops

5. Even human decay is brought into the realm of "culture" through the doctrine of bodily resurrection, which will occur when the world is perfected according to God's moral code.

to feed themselves and their cattle (Leviticus 26:4; Deuteronomy 11:14); and through the characterization of the Promised Land as "a land of hills and valleys [that] soaks up its waters from the rains of heaven" (Deuteronomy 11:11).

The desert is a place bounded by water—God parts the Red Sea, the Israelites cross the Jordan into Canaan—but containing no potable water itself, unless it has been sent, or unless brackish water has been converted into potable water, by God. Even Egypt is more fertile than the wilderness. The Israelites complain angrily to Moses and Aaron:

> Why have you brought the Lord's congregation into this wilderness for us and our beasts to die here? Why did you make us leave Egypt to bring us to this wretched place, a place with no green or vines or pomegranates? There is not even water to drink! [Numbers 20:4–5]

> If only we had meat to eat! We remember the fish that we used to eat free in Egypt, the cucumbers, the melons, the leeks, the onions, and the garlic. Now our gullets are shriveled. There is nothing at all! Nothing but this manna to look to! [Numbers 11:4]

In the wilderness, the Jews meet a side of nature they cannot dominate: the desert is a place where survival depends on the acceptance of subservience. They may argue with God about their existence in the barren desert, but they must not doubt God's divine plan and providence if they are to reach the Promised Land. Because they doubt, God punishes the people with disease and death. The elders die in the desert, and Moses loses his right to cross into Canaan (Numbers 20:2–3).

More than representing a physical location, the desert is a state of redefinition and purification for the Israelites. In the sparse and sunlit desert, they face the limits of their human condition and the supremacy of God, both in the laws that control the society and in the laws that control the natural world. This recognition of their relationship to nature turns them toward the Promised Land.

The supreme moment of unity between desert and culture comes with the giving of the Law on the mountain of Sinai. At Sinai, God is the Nature that is beyond "culture": he appears in natural forms, thunder and lightning, which suggest nature as repetitious and powerful, and not subject to the disintegration of animal or plant life. It is the nature of the principles of universal heavenly order, the Seder, that appears at Sinai: nature in its eternal form, the nature of the desert. In the desert man acquires the means of comprehending the stability that lies beyond his own decay. At its most extreme, man's "culture" melts into natural law.

Sinai and Sabbath are the most extreme expressions of the unity of God and man in Judaism. Sinai signifies the highly rational comprehension of the Divine Order that is the quest of each devout Jew; Sabbath, "the day of holy unity," "the day of the covenant," is enveloped in the more emotional imagery of Shekinah and God, Community of Israel and God, and is accompanied with sensual rituals of light, song, and food, as well as being a day of study. Man may use the concept of the ideal feminine as Shekinah and Torah, but his aim on the Sabbath is the same as at Sinai: to go beyond the change and dissolution of that nature which man tries to control in order to meet the eternal face of Nature.

The laws of the Sabbath that prohibit work closely follow the logic of Lévi-Strauss's distinction between "nature" and "culture." "Work" is defined as anything that imposes transformation upon the material world, not as energy expended. Therefore, no raw food may be cooked, no fire started, no object brought from a resting state to an active one (thus, no car may be started). Food already cooked may be kept warm, but cold food may not be heated. On the Sabbath, the Jew returns to a "natural," nonmastery state, one freed from considerations of change and transformation. Once the guidelines for the Sabbath are in order, the Law is no longer a working social tool but an ideal path to meeting God.

The two white foods of the desert, manna and matzah, express in inverse form this communication between heaven and earth. Manna falls from God as a natural food, sweet, flaky, "like wafers in honey," and is subject to decomposition if it is not gathered as God directs. Matzah is a perfected cultural product, unseasoned, hard, and lasting. Made and eaten according to the directions in the Torah and in accordance with later traditions, matzah expresses man's conformity to God's will. If manna is an offering from God to man, matzah is an offering of acquiescence from man to God.

As a product made in strict obedience to the laws of "culture," matzah is a metaphor for the priestly people themselves, an extension of the fundamental metaphoric relationship between bread and man found in talmudic thought.

The Talmud (Berakhot 61a and elsewhere) speaks of two inclinations placed in man's heart by God: the *yetzer hatov,* the good, and the *yetzer hara,* the evil. The presence of evil on earth is understood as part of God's creation and divine plan, not as a counterforce to God, despite the occasional personification of evil as "Satan": "I form the light, and create the darkness; I make peace, and create evil" (Isaiah 24:7).

According to the Midrash, the rabbinic interpretations that are meant to elucidate the Mishnah, the *yetzer hara* is a potential for evil, not a determinant of man's actions. It can be countered and mastered by obedience to the Law: "The evil *yetzer* does not walk at the side, but in the middle of the street. . . . If the *yetzer* comes and would jest with you, drive it away with words of Torah. . . . In yourself should be your trust" (Isaiah 26:3; cf. *Genesis, Rabah,* Bereshit 22, 6). Man's duty is to confront, acknowledge, and master evil, not lock himself away from temptation. This ability to make decisions about his actions and to overcome the evil inclination constitutes man's free will. Evil in the universe is not so much a pull away from good as it is a condition for it, and the choice of paths is up to man.

The Talmud calls the evil impulse "leaven" in the sense of fermenting passion (Berakhot 17a), and the Midrash develops the connection: "So God said: 'It was I who put the bad leaven in the dough, for the *yetzer* of the heart of man is evil from his youth' " (*Tanhuma, Bereshit,* Noah, 15b), and "Poor must be the dough, which the Baker himself calls evil" (*Genesis, Rabah,* Noah, 34, 10). Therefore, the conscious avoidance of leaven and the use of unleavened bread are expressive of the state of moral perfection for which man strives.

The desert experience of the Israelites gave them the Law that defined them as a priestly people and gave the Jews for all time the means for communal and private perfection. At the same time, because man's total perfection would confound the distinction between man and God and is therefore impossible, human realization of perfection is ultimately elusive. Man tries, but necessarily fails. In his stead, he can make wheat and water conform to an ideal of perfection and stay in a pure, priestly state.

At the Temple, the relationship between matzah and priests was acknowledged in the proscription of leavened bread to the priest at the High Altar. No offering of meal could contain leaven; a portion of the flour and oil was salted and then burned, and the remainder was eaten by the priests in the form of unleavened bread. "What is left of it shall be eaten by Aaron and his sons; it shall be eaten as unleavened cakes, in the sacred precinct; they shall eat it in the enclosure of the Tent of Meeting. It shall not be baked with leaven . . ." (Leviticus 6:9–10). As long as the Temple stood, the sacrifices of meal and meat were the means through which man communicated with God.

In present times, the leaven placed on the windowsills of the home during the Search for Leaven acts as an "impurity" on the boundaries of the community. When the priest-father takes the leaven outside the house, he is thus metaphorically cleansing society itself. The passage of time between the last eating of leaven at breakfast on the morning before Passover and the first taste of matzah at the Seder clears the body of leaven's "impurity" as the house has been cleared. Both "houses" are made ready to receive the pure matzah that defines the time as especially sacred.

As with the Search for Leaven, community and individual perfection is conveyed through the casting out of leavened bread at the ceremony of *Tashlikh*. On the afternoon of Rosh Hashana, the Jew walks together with other members of the community to the edge of a stream, preferably outside the city limits, shakes the edges of his garments, and turns his pockets inside out to indicate casting his sins into the purifying waters. It has become the custom to carry bits of bread to toss in the flowing stream to the accompaniment of the words from Micah 7:19: "Thou wilt cast all our sins into the depths of the sea" and "Cast away from yourselves all your transgression, and create within yourselves a new heart and a new spirit." Like the Seder and the Search for Leaven, *Tashlikh* is a creation of the Jews of the diaspora, probably dating from the fourteenth century.

At the Seder, matzah is called the "bread of affliction" and is raised up for all to see. This presents a paradox: "up" is a direction of honor in Judaism, (see chapter 8), and yet affliction, suffering, has never been an honored state in Judaism. In this apparently simple action, the Seder crystallizes the contrasts and conflicts present throughout the entire ceremony.

While the Seder is convened to retell the story of the Exodus, which was preceded by the Paschal sacrifice, it is the matzah, and not the meat, that is to be eaten during Passover. Instead of consuming the sacrifice as the last food in the celebration, the matzah, as *afikoman,* is the final food of the Seder. By placing the focus on the matzah that was carried into the desert, the Seder turns its attention to the period of time between leaving Egypt and arriving in Jerusalem. It was then that the people, like children reaching adulthood, were opened to the possibility of special honor through the Law, as well as to the possibility of failure. As all stretch out their hands to help support the raised matzah, they honor the past existence in the desert and their own present state as well.

The interplay between matzah and wine, then, is really between fundamental coordinates of Jewish culture. Matzah speaks of stability, eternal promise, purity, the priestly nature of the community, and man's ability to control and order. It suggests the permanence of the everlasting covenant and also the permanence of the Jew's desert existence between Egypt and Jerusalem. The wine, however, suggests more earthy, transitory matters—sensuous pleasure, fellowship, human life itself. Matzah and wine define the boundaries of the Jew's existence between that which can be made "cultural" but never really controlled, like the endlessly fermenting wine, and that which allows man to exhibit "culture" in a form approximating the immutability of God's Law, the matzah. Both matzah and wine express the individual and collective hopes and experiences of the Jew. They are together on the table, as in daily life, but by separating them—covering and uncovering the matzah, the mandatory drinking of the wine—each element is allowed its own voice.

While within the Jewish universe all items become "culture" through definition and control, some things come to represent the ideal more perfectly on the "nature"-to-"culture" continuum. Matzah is man's most perfected form, his closest counterpart to God's representation on earth, the Torah. Represented graphically, with highest perfection at the right, the path from "nature" to "culture" is shown in table 7.

TABLE 7.

The path from "nature" to "culture": social creation in Jewish life.

Nature	Imperfect Transformations	Culture
uncircumcised males, infants	children, uncircumcised mature males (arals)	adult males
permitted animal life	ritually slaughtered, salted, soaked meat	cooked meat
flour and water	leavened bread	matzah
fruit before the fourth year	fruit after the fourth year	
	wine	
	women	
	home	synagogue (Torah)

The benedictions said over foods recognize the natural and imposed transformations discussed in this chapter. All foods eaten in the raw state are first given one of the following benedictions: "Blessed art Thou, O Lord our God, King of the Universe, who creates the fruit of the ground" *(borey pere ha-adamah)* is said for vegetables; and "Blessed art Thou, O Lord our God, King of the Universe, who creates the fruit of the tree" *(borey pere ha-atz)* is said for fruit.

Once obviously transformed from the natural state, whether salted, cooked, or rotted, the food takes the *Shehakol* blessing: "Blessed art Thou, O Lord our God, by whose word all things exist." In this benediction, creation as a transformation through the divine word is related to the most ordinary activities of the day, the eating of a plate of vegetables or a piece of chicken.

Bread and wine, as encompassing symbols and not specific items, have their own, separate benedictions. Bread represents sustenance itself, and its benediction, "Blessed art Thou, O Lord Our God, who brings bread from the earth," sanctifies the entire meal. Wine is also used at the start of a festival meal to indicate God's goodness and bounty, and it too is honored independently with its own benediction, "Blessed art Thou, O Lord Our God, who creates the fruit of the vine."

Through the intrusion of the Law, animal, vegetable, and human life become social products. The transformation of each of them to conform to the Law is evidence of an underlying system of structured thought. Neither dietary nor social relationships are prior to or causative of relations on another level; rather, each set of patterns that emerges from the material of everyday life is evidence of inherent organizing principles of discernment and categorization, and each set of homologous relationships robs social experience of some of its chaos and fear.

6
History As Myth

Both [music and mythology] are instruments
for the obliteration of time.
  Claude Lévi-Strauss
  The Raw and the Cooked

The Seder works with time on many levels, presenting the
Exodus from Egypt as a historical event as well as a paradigmatic sequence explaining the experience of the Jew for all times. The Exodus
is both history, a sequence of events, and myth, a timeless explanatory
model for the society's existence, and this "mythical history" is made
objective and palpable through the objects and actions of the ritual.

History, in Jewish thought, is a purposeful movement toward the
future, and the promise of man's triumph over wickedness and his
return to the Promised Land structures the perception of events. God's
warning to the Jews that "You must not go back that way [to Egypt]
again" (Deuteronomy 17:16), coupled with golden promises of the abundant life to come in the land of milk and honey, firmly anchors the
Exodus and the Jews in history and gives the desert, transition, a historical location. But because the forward progression from Egypt to Jerusalem is commanded by God, the Jews' place in history also has a moral
dimension.

At the Seder, as long as the focus is on the sequential ordering of
events, "history" exists. However, when the view shifts, even slightly,
so that this social construction is a semantic universe that influences
behavior, "history" becomes "myth."

As myth, the historical process from deliverance to redemption is
comprehended in its totality, not just as a sequence of events of which

the present is the middle term, but as a set of relationships that, through metaphoric associations, synthesize the synchronic and diachronic perceptions of time. Lévi-Strauss's words on mythical history seem particularly applicable to Exodus and the Seder:

> Mythical history thus presents the paradox of being both disjoined and conjoined with the present. It is disjoined from it because the original ancestors were of a nature different from contemporary men: they were creators and these are imitators. It is conjoined with it because nothing has been going on since the appearance of the ancestors except events whose recurrence periodically effaces their particularity. . . .
>
> Thanks to ritual, the "disjoined" past of myth is expressed, on the one hand, through biological and seasonal periodicity and, on the other, through the "conjoined" past, which unites from generation to generation the living and the dead. [1970b:236]

The covenant that "conjoins" society and God at Sinai conjoins myth and history; God intrudes into history and eternalizes it. This mythical history is enacted at the Seder in fulfillment of the line "in every generation each Jew must regard himself as though he, personally, were brought out of Egypt. . . ." The "as though" makes it clear that the Seder is not to be understood as a re-enactment of the historical moment of deliverance but as an identification with those who were delivered. The ritual has excluded the primary symbol that would have spoken of a recreation of the historical past, the sacrifice itself, and has substituted a symbol that expresses an identification with the mythical dimension of the story. The matzah suggests a state of being in relation to God. Other objects and images, which also appear as references to history—the bitter herbs, the salt water, the Plagues—simultaneously are references to myth, to the timeless but present situation of the group at the table. The sequential movement of the evening parallels the historical account: first the Haggadah extols the deliverance, then it convenes a communal meal in the present, and finally it calls for redemption. However, at each stage the action reminds both the participants and God of the eternal promises of the covenant, and so turns history into myth.

This sense of unity of past, present, and eternal time begins with the assumption by the Haggadah of leadership at the Seder. Although each father is called the leader at his own Seder, it is the Haggadah, with its quotations from the Torah, its hymns of praise to God, and its instructions for the use of the symbolic foods, that directs the evening's activities. The leader acts as priest, carrying out these instructions, raising, lowering, reclining, eating, singing, even if others fail to do so. Yet, he is more an exemplary man than a controller. Although the Haggadah is not regarded as divine in origin, as is the Torah, still the individual's relationship to the texts is similar. The Jew is responsible for implementing the divine plan in the Torah, but the ultimate design is not his. Men may have compiled the Haggadah, but it relates to a divinely inspired historical process that governs each person. A Yiddish proverb says succinctly, "Man drives, but God holds the reins." In history, as in the Haggadah, man has freedom of will and movement—even freedom to disobey—but within a preconditioned framework.

The treatment in the Haggadah of the "leader" of the Exodus, Moses, is illustrative of the position of the "leader" at the Seder. In Exodus, Moses is God's often recalcitrant instrument; his great acts come not by his own will, but when he recognizes and accedes to God's will. Moses is a great man shown with all the human failings of impatience, anger, and disobedience. He is more "human" than the ideal man who will be sent to deliver the people in the future, the messiah, but both great deliverers of the Jews contain no divinity themselves and are important only as they serve to move history forward according to God's plan. Moses the leader, Moses the Levite, is not even singled out by name in the Haggadah's glorification of the deliverance; his name is mentioned only once, in an incidental reference from the Book of Exodus. Leaders among men follow, attuned to a consistent imperative. The priests at each Seder see that all present act out their duties.

A distinction is made here between the eternal "music" of the Haggadah, its divine historical tale, to which the company is progressively attuned, and the medium that brings that story home. Respect is given to the spirit of the Haggadah; the paper itself may be ragged and wine-stained, even if it once was gloriously illustrated and finely bound. Such a condition is impossible for the Torah, which, as God's revealed word, is a holy object, set apart, dressed in the finest of fabrics, crowned with silver, the words touched only with a pointer. Each letter must be periodically examined to see that the ink is still perfect. The Torah stays in the synagogue in a place of honor, its own special Ark in the eastern wall. The Haggadah, by contrast, is the work of man, a means to make known to each member of the community the essential visions of the Torah. It is a teaching tool, not the divine word itself, and, like the Seder, may contain appeals to sensual comprehension of the messages of Exodus.

The relationship of the Haggadah to the Torah is somewhat similar to the relationship of the "Haggadah" portion of the Talmud to the rest of the work. Both Haggadahs are collections of legend and informal knowledge used to illustrate important principles. Despite its order, the art, legends, and ease of handling make the Haggadah appropriate for the less tutored, as well as to the less formal spirit of the Seder.

Although there are variations in the visual presentation of the Haggadah, certain readings and instructions for action are the same the world over, and these core sections form the order that unites all groups through space and time.

The Haggadah divides the ritual into three main parts along a historical axis. The first and oldest part of the Haggadah deals with the deliverance from Egypt and explains the causes for celebration. The middle section is the meal. The final part speaks mostly of hopes of future deliverance, with hymns of praise to God and the welcoming of the forerunner of the messiah, Elijah. After the Seder proper, there are traditional songs and readings.

In locating the meal between past and future, the Haggadah reinforces the sense of present communion as part of a historical process, in between past slavery and future redemption. The celebrants eat together, just as Moses and the elders ate a communal meal on Mount Sinai after the Israelites had demonstrated with sacrifices their acceptance of the covenant and after they had been wet with the "blood of the covenant" (Exodus 24:5–11).

The meal is made to appear as the midway point between the initial and concluding sections by the balanced use of the cups of wine. Most of the action takes place in the beginning; it is in this section, much longer than the conclusion, that all the symbolic foods are pointed out and discussed, and the significant readings about the matzah and the children take place. In each section, however, two of the four mandatory cups of wine are drunk. Spaced this way, they call attention to and make necessary the completion of the Seder despite the very late hour.

The Seder is a dialogue with God, or, rather, one side of the argument. It presents conditions on earth as the participants see them. While the tone throughout the Haggadah is glorificatory, the praises are interspersed with reminders to God that for the present generation the process of liberation has not yet been completed. The society demon-

strates that it is fulfilling its obligations under the covenant while it
reminds God of his; the Seder concludes with the words: "The Seder of
the Passover is now complete according to the laws, rules and customs.
. . . Next year in Jerusalem!"[1] The society, the Haggadah is saying, is
doing its part. Now it is God's move. The Seder ends with a singing,
laughing community awaiting God's response.

As the Seder takes the assembly through history as chronology, it
simultaneously collapses the chronology into the present and relates the
present and the eternal. Although many metaphoric means are used to
achieve this unity, it is primarily through the use of the two languages
of the Haggadah (not including the vernacular), Hebrew and Aramaic,
that this synthesis takes place.

As discussed before, language has been understood as a potent
force that has transformatory power as well as the power to actualize
the meanings behind the sound. Sound and meaning are not easily
separated; the word is the presence, the name is the person, the Torah
is the seat of God's Indwelling, or Shekinah. The very observant Jew will
not write any of God's "names" on a paper that might someday be
defaced or destroyed; instead he uses a form such as "G-d." Jewish
magic has frequently employed phrases from the Bible to invoke God's
protection or help. Names in particular could conjure up power, and by
the Middle Ages all words, all incantations, were understood as names
capable of calling forth and unleashing forces on earth. God's "name"
or "names" are still the focus of the mystical strain in Judaism, and the
Talmud and the Kabbala both discuss the many possible names for God
as a means of comprehending and approaching his essence. The Spanish
kabbalist of the Middle Ages, Moses de Leon, wrote that the entire
Torah is composed of the single and holy mystical name of God, and the
founder of the Hasidic movement, the Baal Shem Tov, proposed that
the Torah originally consisted of a jumble of letters, phrases, chapters,
and sentences that fell into order when the events they describe actually took place. The letters and the punctuation of the Torah, therefore,
express the divine energy of creation, and hence cannot be changed or
touched.

Words might have the power to effect the very state being discussed, and so any mention of evil, such as death or illness, is qualified
by a protective phrase, such as "God forbid." An explanation for this

1. Those already in Israel say, "Next year in Jerusalem rebuilt!"

practice, still present in common speech, comes from popular folklore, which pictures God surrounded by angels zealous to do his bidding. Sometimes the angels mistake a human voice for that of God and rush to carry out ideas expressed by man. Spoken words, therefore, can be taken out of context by the angels, with dire consequences.

While in all languages spoken words must be handled with care, and phrases containing unpleasant thoughts can be negated by one invoking divine protection, Hebrew above all other languages is expressive of the divine. As the Talmud says, "A covenant is made with the lips" (Mo'ed Katan 18a).

Like all sacred languages, Hebrew opens communication with another realm of space and time. This perception of Hebrew as immediate communication caused trouble at the time of the founding of the State of Israel. There was, and is, strong opposition to the use of Hebrew as a national language, open to secular and thus potentially defiling referents and contexts. While many see the revival of spoken Hebrew as the revitalization of an ancient people and a step toward the realization of the promise in Exodus, others see the secular use of Hebrew as a profanation of the sacred tongue and inappropriate until the coming of the messiah. These groups continue to use Yiddish, or another tongue, as their daily language, even if they live in Israel. Hebrew's eternal dimension intrudes on daily life in every prayer and benediction. To conduct a Seder in Hebrew, therefore, is to place the ceremony outside ordinary conceptions of time and to make the history being told part of the experience of the divine.

This sense of "divine history" is recognized in the synagogue by continual study of the Hebrew Torah. In the home, however, stories are more usually told in one of the many vernaculars used by the Jews. A fully Hebrew ceremony in the home makes "this night different," and even where the ceremony is conducted in the vernacular for people who do not fully understand Hebrew, some Hebrew is retained at crucial points, often in a form in which all can join. There may be transliteration, and the benedictions and choruses of the songs are in a simple, repetitive Hebrew that even the youngest child (or the woman) can learn and echo. Thus, no one is kept from uttering a few sacred words.

Aramaic, the other language of the Haggadah, has both a historical and an eternal dimension. Aramaic was the vernacular of ancient Israel, used during the Babylonian exile, the period of the second Temple, and the following centuries. This was the time during which the Talmud was developed as a means of interpreting the Torah for use in new historical circumstances. By the ninth century Arabic had replaced Aramaic as the vernacular of the Jews of the Middle East, and Aramaic became a holy language second only to Hebrew. Sometime about the thirteenth century in Spain, the principal book of Jewish mysticism, the Zohar, was written in Aramaic. Through the language, European mystics expressed their participation in the mystical tradition begun in Babylonia.

As the language of mysticism, Aramaic is expressive of the personal relationship between man and God. This is a relationship of even more immediacy than is expressed in Hebrew. Hebrew expresses the relationship of a people to God: one reaches God and achieves salvation through communal laws as given by God in Hebrew. Mysticism in general by-passes the interposition of the laws and authority of the community, as in a priesthood, and places the individual in a one-to-one, "I and Thou" relationship with God. Within Judaism, the mystical sense of Aramaic as private communication is tempered by having all prayers phrased, like Hebrew ones, in the collective, by locating them within the predominantly Hebrew liturgy, and by confining such prayers to times when a special need to express immediacy is felt. In this way, the sense of heightened closeness is kept a communal experience. On the afternoon of the "day of unity," the Sabbath, the day when each man is said to have an "extra soul," men sit together around the luncheon table singing Aramaic "table hymns," a custom begun over two thousand years ago.

Aramaic is often used in Judaism to express the more immediate relationship between man and God made possible in transitional periods, a relationship that also suggests special protection. The time when one's past is being judged and the future decided, the Day of Atonement, begins with the chanting of the Aramaic prayer *Kol Nidré* ("All Vows"). At Shavuot, the festival commemorating the transition from Israelite wanderers to Jewish people, the revelation at Mount Sinai, the Aramaic *Akdamut* hymn is sung. The marriage contract, the *ketuba*, has kept its original Aramaic form, as has the divorce agreement, the *get*. The transition from child to adult is still called by its Aramaic name, the *Bar Mitzvah*, and at the funeral and on the anniversary of the death of a parent, the Jew chants the Aramaic *Kaddish* prayer of praise to God.

Aramaic frames the Seder and illuminates its pivotal theme. It is the removal of leaven above all else that sets the very sacred days of

Passover apart from the rest of the year, and this separation is voiced in Aramaic. The final disposition of the leaven before Passover begins with a declaration, in Aramaic, at the end of the ritual search for leaven, that all the leaven is gone. The next morning the final burning of the leaven is also accompanied by Aramaic words, and the Seder concludes with the raucous singing of a "child's" tune, the allegorical *Chad Gadya*, in Aramaic.

The Seder as a drama of present passage as well as a recollection of a past "night of watching" is expressed through the key reading, in Aramaic, the *HaLachma Anya*. Its recitation is crucial to the comprehension of the Seder, since it is during the recitation that the matzah is raised and the words "Lo, this is the bread of affliction" are pronounced. The *HaLachma Anya* is believed to be one of the oldest portions of the Haggadah, dating back to the sixth century B.C.E., the period of the Babylonian exile. The Aramaic words not only refer to this event in history but reinforce the identity of the present period of exile in Europe, Asia, the Middle East, or anywhere else the Seder is enacted, with the exile in Babylonia. Furthermore, the Aramaic of the *HaLachma Anya* identifies the participants at the Seder with the persons in Babylonia in the lines:

> This year we are here, next year we will be in Israel.
> This year we are slaves, next year we shall be free men.

The parallel structure of these lines suggests that here = slaves, Israel = free men.

After this identification through Aramaic, the Haggadah returns to Hebrew in the Four Questions of the child, and then in the lines:

> We were Pharaoh's slaves in Egypt. But the Lord our God brought us out of there with a mighty hand and an outstretched arm. . . .

The Seder thus establishes an identification with a past exile followed by the questioning of a child about his history and customs and a firm declaration of God's goodness and his act of deliverance. The two communal readings say, "we are slaves" and "we were slaves," we are not yet free and we are free, an indeterminate, inconclusive state that expresses the present's comprehension of *galut*. [2]

2. The recitation of the "we are slaves" passage in Aramaic and the identification of the present state of exile with that of Babylonia make an "erroneous" footnote in van Gennep's *Rites of Passage* not quite so incorrect after all. Recognizing that Passover occurs in the early spring, van Gennep suggested that it is a rite of passage and connected the festival with the exit of the Jews from Babylonia (1969:40). Van Gennep correctly identified the spirit of the holiday, if not the letter.

Aramaic is used to express the timeless state of *galut,* the eternal situation of indetermination implicit in a covenant that demands subservience from man but allows him free will and that demands his perfection but reserves perfection for God; Hebrew places that timeless state in history by declaring that Egypt is in the past. As long as Egypt is in the past, so is utter despair. Exile is further infused with a spirit of hope through the positioning of the Four Questions between the Aramaic and Hebrew proclamations of the state of exile. The two passages are separated by the questioning, morally aware child who, as the next chapter will show more fully, suggests the possibility that the Jew is able to hasten his own redemption through knowledge.

Music, like Aramaic, has been used as a nonmediated, nonrational pathway to the divine to complement the rationality of the Torah service and daily life. This relationship, established in the time of the Temple through the bells on the robe of the High Priest and the singing of the Psalms, has been continued in the synagogue with the chanting of the Torah. Some congregations employ professional cantors and choirs, but the very pious still sway to a hidden rhythm as they pray. The mystics developed a great body of hymns, some of which have entered the liturgy; the hymn welcoming the "Sabbath Bride" is widely used. One of the purest expressions of music as an emotional, nondivisible state beyond the temporal is the *niggun,* a wordless tune articulated only through nonsense syllables such as "bom," "bim," and "ya-ba-bim," sung over and over, on and on, as Hasidic scholars sit together. The Hasidic rabbi Schneur Zalman of Liadi expressed the relation of music to words in this way: "Melody is the speech of the soul, but words interrupt the stream of emotion" (Binder 1971:183).

Words exist as differentiation, distinctions, through which one can rationally comprehend meanings; music is a more direct, noncognitive path to the same source. Music has become a metaphor for the Sabbath state of unity between heaven and earth, as in the words of this contemporary song by the Hasidic folksinger Shlomo Carlebach, inspired by Psalm 92, the "Song for the Sabbath Day":

> The whole world is waiting to sing a song of Sabbath
> And I am also waiting to sing a song of Sabbath.
> The flowers and the trees sing a song of Sabbath,
> The valleys and the mountains sing a song of Sabbath.
> The stars in the sky sing a song of Sabbath,
> The angels in heaven sing a song of Sabbath.

I saw six million dying, they sang a song of Sabbath.
I heard their last will crying, sing a song of Sabbath.
Stop all this hatred, sing a song of Sabbath.
Love one another, sing a song of Sabbath.
Dance in the streets, sing a song of Sabbath.[3]

The ultimate paean to unification is the Song of Songs, in which words are used to develop an emotional, sensuous imagery. The Shekinah's approach is described by the Talmud as being announced by the tinkling of an ethereal bell. And redemption itself will be accompanied by joyful singing, as was the first redemption. Miriam, Moses, and all the Israelites sang praise to God when they reached the far shore of the Red Sea, and in the future, "the ransomed of the Lord shall return, and come singing into Zion, and everlasting joy shall be upon their heads" (Mekhilta, Beshallah, 1). Hasidic lore has many references to song and dance as a divine medium. One recounts how the Baal Shem Tov first danced with his congregation, then with the Torah, and then laid the scrolls down and danced alone. His disciples then said: "Now our master has laid aside the visible, dimensional teachings, and has taken the spiritual teachings unto himself " (Buber 1975:53).

In the Torah, and still today, the immediate presence of God and the purification of man's soul are thought to be announced by the sounds of the natural trumpet, the ram's horn, or *shofar.* The revelation at Mount Sinai is proclaimed by the sound of the *shofar* (Exodus 19:16), as is God's return to the heavenly spheres once he has provided mankind with his continual presence, his Word: "The Lord is gone amidst the sound of the horn" (Psalms 47:6). The conclusion of the days of repentance is marked by the sound of the *shofar,* and the *shofar* will herald the beginning of the messianic days; God himself will sound the *shofar* to begin the Ingathering of the Exiles and the resurrection of the dead.

This comprehension of the presence of the divine in the instrument culturally fashioned from nature found its practical application in the folklore of the Middle Ages. Blowing the *shofar* at the conclusion of Yom Kippur was believed to drive off evil spirits, and one curative spell invoked seven angels, patriarchs, altars, heavens, suns, moons, names of God, and *shofars.* Jewish magic never opposed or attempted to subvert the religious system. Rather, it tried to harness

3. Quoted with the publisher's permission from *The Shlomo Carlebach Songbook II* (Cedarhurst, N.Y.: Tara Publications, 1980), p. 77.

the power suggested by the religion; thus, seven *shofars,* like seven heavens, might invoke even more of God's power in the war against disease.

The sound of the *shofar* and the meaningless sounds of the *niggun* are the most extreme expression of music as a nonrationalized path to God. Still, for the Hasidim in particular, man's quest is for the essence behind the words of the Torah, beyond sound itself. When the Hasid says that words are like the outer garments of the Torah and meanings must be peeled away like layers of an onion, one must ask what lies at the core. The ultimate quest here leads not to a void but to an undifferentiated realm of purity and goodness, a realm of potent silence. Martin Buber discusses this realm in describing the Hasidic conception of the biblical prophet: "To be the *nabi* [prophet] of an Elohim [a power, that is, God] thus means to be his 'mouth.' His mouth, not his mouthpiece: the *nabi* does not convey a finished speech that has already become audible; rather he shapes to sound a secret, soundless speech, in the human sense, preverbal, in the divine, primordially verbal, as the mouth of a person shapes to sound the secret, soundless speech of his innermost being" (1966:156). As much as he might seek to experience this hidden dimension of existence, the Jew's life is never focused solely on this realm. The call of the *shofar* does not remind the Jew of his need for contemplation but of his need to repent, and repentance is evidenced not by thought but by deed.

In Jewish life, music joins with words, as woman joins with man, to provide an experience of unity in the approach to, and confrontation with, God. Despite the fact that women's public ritual activities were very circumscribed during the time of the compilation of the original Code of Jewish Law (as opposed to Ganzfried's abbreviation of it), this guide does permit women to blow the *shofar* (Orah Hayyim 589:6).

The sounds of the *shofar* and singing proclaim resolution with God, both as the moral perfection of Yom Kippur and Sinai, and as unity in the Promised Time and Land, as on the far shore of the Red Sea, and at the start of the messianic days. These vibrant noises proclaim the end of a period of transition, in daily life and ideal construction. At the conclusion of the Seder, the loud singing similarly announces the end of the "desert" state of the evening, and, like the songs of the Israelites at the Red Sea, expresses a successful passage.

The mythical invades the historical present through sequencing, language, and song, but also through images and action. For instance, the Ten Plagues—or, more exactly, the Ten Blows—appear to refer completely to a time long past, and their recitation, and the spilling of wine that accompanies the sounding of each plague, appear to be purely acts of commemoration. A closer analysis, however, shows that the plagues not only describe events in Egypt but also taboos or states feared by both the Israelites and the present community. The names of the plagues are not merely descriptive of material occurrences in Egypt, but also, as symbols, suggest concepts whose presence in words threatens the present community either by conjuring up parts of nature placed outside the bounds of society or by suggesting the society's destruction.

The actions that accompany the sounding of each plague have been given a range of interpretations, from the ecumenical to the prophylactic. Despite the divine protection believed to to be present on this "night of watching," the Talmud records, and later folk beliefs point to, an appreciation of the protective function of the acts for the present community.

The words that generate this anxiety are:

Blood—as the life force, it must be handled with extreme care, controlled. It carries a taboo according to dietary law.

Lice—swarming insects, prohibited by dietary law.

Frogs—prohibited by dietary laws.[4]

Wild beasts—animal life not included in the covenant and so not "inside," domestic creatures. Therefore, "outside," "alien," "not civilized," "predatory." All animals that cannot be slaughtered according to dietary laws are taboo.[5]

Pestilence—actually "cattle disease," feared by Israelite herders; through the identification of man and animal, "blemished," "impure."

Boils—a blemish, an impurity.

4. Douglas says frogs are permitted according to the Law (1970:71), referring to a notation in the Mishnah that lists frogs with creeping things and allows them. In Europe, however, frogs were prohibited. Practice in the Middle Ages became more rigid to ensure every possible compliance with the law.

5. Jewish children are admonished in Yiddish not to act like a *vilda chaya*, a wild beast.

Hail—"wild nature," uncontrolled, a danger to domestic crops; an ambiguous category, neither snow nor rain.

Locusts—taboo according to dietary laws;[6] a plague to domestic crops. In this sense, they are "wild animal life."

Darkness—absence of light (God, Torah).

Slaying of the first-born—a practice of sacrifice outlawed by the Israelites. Israel is called the "first-born son of God," and therefore the slaying of the first-born suggests the destruction of Israel.

At the recitation of each plague, the participant dips his finger into the wine and shakes some wine onto his plate, or spills a few drops, to diminish his cup of joy "in memory of the slain Egyptians." Proverbs 24:17–18 is quoted at this point:

> Rejoice not when your enemy falls,
> And let not your heart be glad when he stumbles;
> Lest the Lord see it, and it displease Him,
> And He turn away His wrath from him.

A legend from the Talmud is also told: "When the Egyptians were drowning in the Red Sea, God restrained his angels from singing his praise, saying: 'How can you sing while my creatures are drowning in the sea?' " (Mequillo 10b).

Spilling wine from the cup of joy is also consistent with the presence, through language, of that which threatens the safety of the community. Wine poured on the ground was a common folk practice throughout the Middle Ages to appease the negative forces, the demons, who might threaten the happiness of those in transitional, vulnerable states. At a wedding, wine was poured on the ground to placate the demons and neutralize their effects, and some of the wine of the *Havdalah* ceremony separating the protected holy day from the rest of the week was also spilled on the ground. Even now, the cup of wine at *Havdalah* is deliberately filled to overflowing (this is explained as "overflowing joy"). Sephardic custom echoes this protective function of the wine. Many Sephardim mix the wine spilled during the recitation of the

6. The laws of Leviticus permit some types of locust to be eaten. Later authorities in Europe banned all locusts, citing the impossibility of avoiding errors in distinguishing between permitted and forbidden types (although the association of locusts, plagues, and Egypt may have played a part). Among Yemenite Jews, who apparently can distinguish among types of locust, some locusts are ground for use as flour.

Ten Plagues with pure water in a basin and then empty it on the ground outside, preferably exiting through the back door. After returning to the house the wife wishes everyone at the table, "Muchos años," "many years," a Judeo-Spanish good luck phrase.

The protective action of spilling the wine is reinforced by spilling more drops of wine at the recitation of the three mnemonic words at the conclusion of the reading of the Ten Plagues. These essentially meaningless words are formed from the initial letters of the Plagues, and are generally explained as an aid to memorizing them, although it is not clear how one remembers meaningless words.[7] Their function seems less a memory aid than a protective device based on the folk beliefs in the magical properties of words and numbers that infuse the recitation of the Ten Plagues.

From ancient times folk belief has considered odd numbers lucky, even numbers dangerous. One was warned against doing two things at one time, repeating an action, marrying two couples on the same day, marrying off two children at one time, and permitting any dual unions within two families, such as two brothers marrying two sisters. The Code of Jewish Law also admonishes that "a man should be careful not to pass between two women, two dogs, or two swine. Nor should two men permit a woman, a dog, or a swine to pass between them" (vol. 1, 3:8). (The relationship between these three beings remains to be examined.)

There is an extensive discussion in Pesahim, the section of the Talmud dealing with the Seder, about the number of cups of wine safe to drink at the ritual. Although ancient practice appeared to dictate four cups of wine, and the presence of four cups is still justified by relating them to the four promises of redemption found in Exodus, the Talmud asks: "How could our Rabbis enact something whereby one is led into danger: surely it was taught: A man must not eat in pairs, nor drink in pairs, nor cleanse (himself) twice. . . . He who drinks in pairs, his blood is upon his own head. . . . R[abbi] Papa said, Joseph the demon told me: For two we kill; for four we do not kill, (but) for four we harm (the drinker) . . ." (109b–110a).

It was decided that one may dare to drink four cups on Passover because "it is a night that is guarded for all time from evil spirits" (109b). Still, despite this demonstration of faith in God's protection, the Talmud

7. An attempt was made in the fourth century to give meaning to the meaningless words, a memory aid to a memory aid. They have been interpreted as "The scorpion stung the uncle," sounds that remain unrelated to the Seder.

suggests that anyone especially vulnerable to attack by demonic forces, such as a sick person, should drink an extra cup of wine this evening, and explains the presence of Elijah's cup as offering that extra measure of protection to the whole community.

If "pairs" are dangerous, odd numbers such as five, but most especially one, three, seven, and nine (the square of three) are auspicious. The mystics conceive of a triple division of the soul and of God's name as a triad, each part representing a different aspect of his nature. The Talmud refers to three archangels, Michael, Gabriel, and Raphael, who are called upon to help in magical actions, although another tradition lists seven archangels. The Torah lists three major festivals and three cities of refuge. One tossed a new infant into the air, heavenward, three times for good luck in medieval Germany, and magical incantations were often said three times, three hours before sunrise, three days before the new moon, or three days in succession. The magical act itself might be performed in three stages or employ three objects, and any experience which was repeated three times was regarded as prophetic. Several "threes" are in the Seder: three symbols to be explained—the bone, matzah, and bitter herbs; three matzahs; three "fours"—the wine, "Four Sons," and "Four Questions"; and three mnemonic words.

Seven has also been used in magic as a sign and instrument of good fortune and protection, and it is found throughout Judaism to indicate the state of closeness with God. The symbol of the Jewish state in ancient and in modern times is the seven-branched candelabrum. The seven blessings recited at weddings are repeated for seven days. The day that the Torah was received at Sinai is called Shavuot, "weeks," and comes seven times seven days, or seven weeks, after Passover. The *brit* takes place after seven healthy days have passed for the child. Festivals such as Passover and Sukkot are seven days in the Torah, and Rosh Hashana, the New Year, is at the time of the seventh moon, or seventh month, in the Hebrew calendar. The mystics speak of "seven heavens," the bride circles the groom seven times, and on the day of Rejoicing of the Torah, Simchat Torah, seven circuits are made of the synagogue with the Torah. The initial period of mourning is also seven days, *shivah,* although sometimes it is shortened to three days. Trachtenberg, who has compiled the apparently definitive list of Jewish magical practices, records this talmudic prescription to cure a tertian fever: "Take seven prickles from seven palmtrees, seven chips from seven beams, seven nails from seven bridges, seven ashes from seven ovens, seven scoops of earth from seven door-sockets, seven pieces of pitch from seven ships, seven handfuls of cumin, and seven hairs from the beard of an old dog, and tie them to the neck-hole of the shirt with a white twisted cord" (1974:119). God's special protection on the night of watching is conveyed through an increased seven: the time of the exodus is set for the fourteenth day of the first month.

God's unmediated presence when the *shofar* is sounded is underscored by the use of auspicious numbers. The city of Jericho fell on the seventh day of the seige by the Israelites, after seven priests made seven circuits of the city blowing seven *shofars* (Joshua 6: 3–20). In Joshua as in Exodus, victory in this world is not a gift of God but a joint venture: the walls topple after the shouts of the people join the blare of the *shofars.* Moses ascends Mount Sinai to meet the revealed God on the third day, at dawn, amid thunder, lightning, dense clouds, and a very loud blast of a horn (Exodus 19:16). On Rosh Hashana the *shofar* is still sounded three times in three triads of notes. One note, *tekiah,* is a single blast, but two of these "notes," *shevarim* ("broken sounds") and *teruah,* are themselves intensifications of the power of three: *shevarim* consists of three short blasts, and *teruah* is a wavering sound of nine staccato notes. This nine-part note lends its name to the New Year observance: Rosh Hashana is sometimes called *Yom Teruah,* the Day of Sounding the *Shofar* (Numbers 29:1). The *shofar* is blown on the first day of the seventh month (the two days of Rosh Hashana are considered one long day), and on Yom Kippur, the tenth day of the seventh month.

Auspicious numbers appear throughout the Yom Kippur liturgy. As daylight disappears, the service for the Day of Atonement is ushered in with the *Kol Nidré* prayer annulling all vows the individual has made concerning himself. The *Kol Nidré* is chanted three times, and there are three ways one may mitigate the severity of God's judgment: *tshuvah* ("return" or penitence), *tefillah* (prayer), and *tzedakah* (charity or deeds of mercy). The penitential period concludes with three professions of faith: the first is recited once, the second three times, and the third seven times. After this comes one long blast of the *shofar* and the shout "Next year in Jerusalem!"

It should be noted that numbers play an extremely important part in the Kabbala and throughout mystical thought. Much is made of the fact that each Hebrew letter also carries a numerical value, and in one system, the *Gematria,* a correspondence is made between words on the basis of their numerical values. To this day, many persons will not eat nuts at the time of repurification, Rosh Hashana and Yom Kippur, because the numerical values of "nuts" and "sin" are almost the same. Relating man's ideas through a system that appears independent of him also appears to give them eternal validity. This use of numbers to express a realm higher than man is reminiscent of Cassirer's characterization of mathematical symbols as an advance over religion, art, and history, and is also found in Lévi-Strauss's discussion of the seemingly eternal form that underlies myth, music, and mathematics.

But the concern with odd and even numbers has a dual face. It is only in connection with the world of man that even numbers appear to be threatening, awakening evil forces and necessitating man's employment of a counterforce. Odd-even concerns disappear in relation to God: God is comprehended as the unity that absorbs opposites,[8] and the fear present in man's world is "awe," a recognition of sacred power, a power that is the potential for good or evil. It is this recognition of power that makes it impossible to pronounce the four letters understood to represent God's name. Because the name is inseparable from the Presence behind it, it is too powerful, too dangerous to utter, and the four sacred letters are voiced instead as "Adonoi" (Lord), sounds unrelated to the script. There are other, less powerful, three- and ten-letter combinations used to refer to God; these words name attributes of God, not the actual being, so they may be spoken with care.

Although pairs are suspect in the earthly existence, the Kabbala posits four worlds, or planes of God's immanence, from the archetypal world of *azilut,* where the unification of the Shekinah and God takes place, to the world of *asiyah,* or world of making or action, where the Shekinah lives with man in exile.

While pairs other than two are problematical in the world of *asiyah,* the number ten appears to have a special status reminiscent of the four cups of wine at the Seder. Both conservatives and liberals compiled the Passover Mishnah; some considered ten and eight dangerous pairs, others did not; some qualified the conditions under which pairs are feared, whether as an eatable, an action· or an object; others resolved a doubt concerning even numbers "stringently" (Pesahim 110b). Yet one scholar specifically excluded ten cups of a liquid: "The

8. Like odd-even distinctions, the divisions of right and left that are the expressions of positive and negative relations in man's life have no reference to God. This point will be discussed more fully in chapter 8; suffice it to say here that while the Talmud and the Kabbala discuss man as having a right and left seat of good and evil influence, the *yetzers,* these dichotomies are meaningless when applied to the nature of God. Ideas such as the "right hand of God" are always understood as a projection of man's universe on the heavenly universe, not a description of God's being.

Sages instituted ten cups in a mourner's house. Now if you should think that ten cups are subject to (the danger of) pairs, how could our Rabbis arise and enact a regulation whereby one is led into danger! But eight are subject to 'pairs' . . . six is subject to 'pairs,' . . . four is subject to 'pairs' " (110a).

The danger suspected in pairs may be mitigated in the case of ten because ten is suggestive of an avenue of communication between man and God and a reminder of God's power over good as well as evil. The Ten Commandments, which create the society, come from God, and the Ten Plagues, which afflicted the Egyptians—and can threaten the community at the Seder—also come from God. The community, in its formal relationship with God, Torah reading and public prayer, is composed of ten men, the *minyan,* "upon whom the Shekinah smiles," and the community searches its collective and individual souls during the ten days of penitence between Rosh Hashana and Yom Kippur. The removal of ten pieces of leaven from the home during the ritual search for leaven before Passover indicates the removal of impurity from the family. It is through the ten emanations of God, the *sefirot,* that Jewish mysticism measures the levels of society's unification with God. Each of the ten *sefirot* is conceived of as a "light," an outpouring from an eternal, constant Source of all energy and matter, and it is only through these manifestations of God as filtered through the four worlds that man may hope to comprehend the nature and qualities of God and his extension into the created universe. The permutations of meanings possible through ten *sefirot,* four worlds, three souls, the various numbers of names and qualities of God are extremely intricate in the Kabbala, but all, like the search for meaning through the numerical equivalents of letters and words, point back to the unification of earthly categories into an indivisible one.

On the tenth day of Tishri, Yom Kippur, the day of the most intense communication with God, the confession of sins, or *Viddui* prayer, is recited ten times. This practice is said to recall the tradition that the High Priest pronounced the name of God ten times when he approached God on behalf of the community. On Rosh Hashana, ten biblical verses mentioning the *shofar,* the *Shofrot,* are read; in the *Shofrot* the number ten is magnified by quoting ten praises to God from Psalm 150. Other portions of the Rosh Hashana liturgy, *Malhuyot* and *Zihronot,* were also developed through the citation of ten biblical verses.

The Seder, as a presentation of concern with the state of being of the present community, must necessarily focus on the dangers to that assembly, at the same time recognizing its communication with and protection by God. At the recitation of the Ten Plagues, each Hebrew word spoken aloud introduces the extraordinary into the community—ten times.

Through the Plagues, the Seder presents the community with some of its core coordinates—the special relation with God, separation, classification, domestication—in a form, an even number, that reminds it of the dangers to these ordering constructs as well as the ultimate source of all danger and safety. Like the four cups of wine, ten utterances may be dared on this protected night, but, as with the fifth cup of wine, a further protective measure is taken by man. As negative phrases are always countered by positive ones, so the Plagues are first countered by spilling a drop of wine at each word, and finally by collapsing their powerful verbal presence from ten into a protective three through the medium of the first letter of each word. Each of the three sounds that obliterate meaning is reinforced by a drop of spilled wine.

At the same time, the ceremony of the Ten Plagues shows man engaged in negating the dangers to the community and thereby demonstrating his awareness and active participation in God's plan. It is only when the Israelites become aware of their plight and initiate action to change it by crying out to God that deliverance begins; at the Seder, the celebrants acknowledge dangers and God's power, and do something about it. As in Egypt, this is the fundamental step on the path to redemption.

Like the other symbols of the Seder, the Plagues serve to make history and myth coincident, and to reinforce the mythical, timeless, explanatory prism of the Exodus sequence. The past, whether in Egypt or at the destruction of the Temple, is understood as emergence from a settled state; the present, whether desert or diaspora, as a state of transition; and the future, as return to the Promised Land, completion. The sequence of the Haggadah, as it shifts its focus from past to present to future, mirrors the historical progression, but the symbolic identifications turn history into myth at each stage. The result is that those at the Seder sit in an eternal present, a moment in history whose meaning has been predefined by the Exodus, although it remains to be defined still further by the contingent circumstances of everyday life. Table 8 presents the mythical history of the Seder as it orders the evening. Each horizontal represents a different historical sequence; each column the metaphoric identifications of the myth that serve to unite present society with all Jewish societies past and future.

TABLE 8.

The mythical history of the Seder.

Past	Present	Future
Egypt	desert	Promised Land
Israel	exile in Babylonia	Israel
Israel	exile in Europe, Middle East, etc.; *galut*	Israel
first part of the Haggadah	communal meal	final section of the Haggadah

7

The Child As Promise

For the Rabbis, of blessed memory, said,
"Let the pure (the children) come and
engage in the study of purity."
Code of Jewish Law

The concept of God's watchfulness alleviates some of the sense of danger associated with transitional periods. It is through the presence of the child at the Seder that transition becomes even more benign, and even a state of promise. If, in talmudic lore, Elijah is the forerunner of the messiah, at the Seder the child becomes the forerunner of Elijah. An analysis of the conceptualization of the child in Jewish culture and at the Seder will demonstrate how this is so.

The transition to the very sacred time of Passover, which started a month or so before the festival, is completed in the sanctification of the wine, a ritual that signals the beginning of all festival meals throughout the year. It is through the actions that immediately follow the benediction of the wine that the leader dramatizes the special nature of the occasion, one reaching for a state even more sacred than that of other festival days.

As he begins the ceremony, the father demonstrates his suitability to introduce those at the table to the ritual by dressing in the white *kittel* and then associates himself with purity by pouring over his hands the water brought to the table by the children. Pouring water from above is an action that relates water's role as purifier to the source of all purity.

There is disagreement in the Haggadahs about whether it is the leader alone or the whole assembly who ought to wash at this point.

Roth states specifically that only the leader should wash (1959:8), but at many Seders, all wash. Either way, the handwashing is a fulfillment of the requirement that hands are to be washed before eating any food that has been dipped in a liquid; the next action is the dipping of the greens in the salt water.[1] Washing is, at the same time, a demonstration of the purified state of the leader and the community. This state will be reinforced later in the ritual with the second collective handwashing. The second time, a benediction is said when the hands are washed since handwashing accompanied by a benediction must immediately precede any meal. Since a "meal" is defined as food that includes bread "at least the size of an egg" (Code of Jewish Law, vol. 1, 40:1), this benediction is necessary before the matzah, bitter herbs, *haroset,* and dinner may be eaten.

The first handwashing forms part of a preparatory sequence that "sets the stage" as one of increased purity in total agreement with the more sacred state of the evening. The sequence begins with the leader's display and assumption of the *kittel,* continues with the handwashing and the immersion of the greens, and ends with the breaking of the *afikoman.* At this point, several changes take place in the relation of the leader to the group and in the character of the group itself.

After he washes his hands, the leader dips the greens in salt water, the "tears of the slaves," and recites the usual benediction over produce before distributing the greens to be eaten. The greens alone, among all the items on the table, appear in their natural state; by immersing them in salt and water the leader transforms them to a purer state consistent with the rest of the foods. (The blessing over the greens also covers the bitter herbs to be eaten later.)

The leader then divides the middle matzah and sets the larger portion aside as *afikoman,* or "dessert." This will be the last food eaten at the Seder, at the very start of the final section of the Haggadah, and is thus necessary for the completion of the ritual. The preparations over, the narrative can now begin. It opens with the display of the matzah, and the invitation to "all who are hungry" to join the Seder.

With the breaking of the *afikoman,* the leader not only invites the interest and participation of the children, but initiates a reversal of roles in which the children, and not the adults, control the completion of the

1. This handwashing is sometimes explained as an atavism, a practice related to the ritual's origins among Middle Eastern peoples who customarily begin a meal with handwashing and with a first course of greens dipped in salt water.

Seder. The children may "steal" the *afikoman* and return it when the leader "finds it missing" after the meal, or the leader himself may hide the *afikoman* for the children to find. In either case, the leader cannot continue with the ritual until the children agree to relinquish the *afikoman.* A common explanation for the stealing of the *afikoman* is that the anticipation of the moment of return keeps the children interested and alert throughout the Seder. It may, but this explanation fails to account for the fact that the *afikoman* is returned at the beginning of the final part of the Seder, often close to midnight, and children are then free to fall asleep during the passages dealing with redemption.

The stealing of the *afikoman* is the beginning of a process of leveling differences among individuals by giving the children a power they do not possess in ordinary time. Children at Seders seem to realize and enjoy their unusual status: this is the one time in the year that the adults —and, in fact, the whole community as represented by the sample at the table—are dependent upon them. Although the *afikoman* will be exchanged for a gift, the children frequently prolong the process of exchange, bargaining for a gift other than the one offered, recognizing implicitly that once the exchange is completed the brief and unusual power they hold over the adults will be neutralized for another year.

The father submits to the child's dawdling because of the relaxed mood of the evening and because he is reluctant to inject an ordinary father-child relationship into the special ritual one. In allowing and recognizing the temporary superiority of the child, however, the father implicitly acknowledges a theme of Exodus that is developed in the Seder: the important role of the children in bringing the community to a state of completion in relation to God. As the children of the Israelites, and not the fathers, complete the journey through the desert and cross into the Promised Land, so the ritual finds its completion through the children.

The assumption of a measure of control by the child comes at the point in the Seder when the narration is about to begin and the primacy of the historical sequence is being acknowledged. The child's role is possible because of the special meanings of "child" in Judaism in general and especially at the Seder. A "child" is, first of all, one untutored in the language of the culture. This understanding is highlighted at the Seder through the child's formal posing of the questions and by the readings about the four sons, all of whom lack knowledge about Judaism. Each son is defined by his attitude toward learning: the wise son asks and learns; the wicked son rejects the teachings;[2] and the naive and simple sons do not know what or how to ask.

The rationale for the Seder is that it is a forum for teaching the story of the Exodus to each child. As a ritual that deepens the child's cultural awareness, the Seder is part of the process of social incorporation that begins at the circumcision and culminates at the *Bar Mitzvah*. The Code of Jewish Law recognizes this function of the Seder as a rite of incorporation by requiring that "children who have reached the age of initiation, that is, who are able to understand," eat the matzah and drink the wine (vol. 3, 119:1). All other prescriptions in Jewish law depend on the achievement of adulthood. At the Seder, it is the state of imperfect knowledge that gives the boy or girl a part in the ritual.

However, at the Seder it is not just the young child who is being informed; all are being taught once again by the Haggadah. "Child," as one unlearned, has an ageless connotation in a culture whose prime value is found in continual study, and at the Seder everyone, young and old, is encouraged to rethink the stories, ask questions, and offer answers. Even the youngest participant can momentarily act as teacher, and his or her demonstration of knowledge is applauded. And even the oldest participant can ask the Four Questions if no young child is present.

No matter what the composition of the group, the "child's part" is a necessary component of the Seder. If no children are present, a woman reads the questions; if no woman, a man; if a man is alone that evening, he recites the questions. By being potentially open to any member of the community, the concept of "child" as one unlearned is extended to all, and this extension is a recognition of the process in which all are involved. The "childlike" state of the Jew is inherent in the meanings of the word *ben* as both "son" and "member," and in the common term for the Jews, the "children of Israel." As it informs the new initiates, the Seder reinforces and intensifies in the elders the lessons learned in previous years. This function of the Seder is seen most clearly in the Seder in Yemen as it was performed prior to the almost complete exodus of Yemeni Jews to Israel when that state was founded. Contrary to otherwise universal tradition, young children were excluded from the Yemenite Seder; the ritual was a convocation of adults, who took all the roles.

A second connotation of "child" is that of one who is pure. The

2. In Haggadahs from the Middle Ages, the wicked son is often depicted in the illustrations as a man of war, a soldier, and the wise son as a scholar.

child is conceived in a woman who is in a state of purity according to the Law, and the child retains this association with purity by being defined as one not fully aware of the Law and so not yet responsible for its infraction. Therefore, the child does not have to repent by fasting on the Day of Atonement nor does he or she have to undergo periodic ritual immersion. At the *brit* the *mohel* can touch the child's blood to his mouth, and the ceremony can be held in the synagogue, because the child is pure. At the Seder, the child demonstrates his relation to purity by carrying the water for ritual handwashing. As they encircle the table with the pitcher and basin, the children enclose the celebrants in a ring of purity.

This state of purity connects the child with ideas of redemption. Both the Talmud and the Zohar imply that children are the "messiahs of mankind," following the phrase in Isaiah 11:6 that describes the World to Come and concludes: "And a little child shall lead them." If knowledge and moral perfection can bring redemption, then the pure children engaging in the study of the Law are the community's hope for the future. "Who brings no children in the world is like a murderer" (Talmud, Yevamot 63b), for he denies a means of communal perfection as well as of continuation. The Zohar equates man's place in the World to Come with his children in this world: "For he who does not beget children in this world is denied all the blissfulness we have mentioned, and he is not privileged to contemplate the glorious effulgence" (Bereshit 66a), and ". . . it is children that make a man worthy of entering [the World to Come]. Hence happy is the man who is blessed with them and who trains them in the ways of Torah" (Bereshit 188a).

By becoming "children" and relearning the story of the Exodus, everyone at the Seder gains a share of the child's purity and is enabled to participate in the process of redemption. At the end of the Seder, all wait for the prophet Elijah, the forerunner of the messiah and the protector of children.

These two functions, or meanings, of "Elijah" added to that of "mouth" or conduit of the divine, place the prophet at both rituals in which the child has a central role. As God's conduit, Elijah provides a protective presence in times of vulnerability and danger: at *Havdalah*, marking the transition from the holy to the ordinary days, at a marriage (Elijah watches over and records all marriages decreed in heaven), at the *brit*, and at the Seder.[3] Elijah is present at the *brit* and the Seder

3. Elijah is not present at the transitional rite of *Bar Mitzvah*, when the more powerful and immediate word of God is present in the Torah.

for the same reasons: because the messiah might appear at any time among the children, and because he protects the individual child at the *brit* and the collective "children" at the Seder.

The relation between the *brit* and the Seder is established also through the meanings evoked by the blood of the newly circumcised child. The drop of blood, without which no *brit* is complete, indicates the relation between child and God, the kin group and God, and the complexes of meanings that make up the *brit* and Seder.

Elijah, the prophet who accompanies the Jews in the *galut,* is at the *brit* when these words from the prophet of the Babylonian exile are said, connecting the *brit* with Passover: "In thy blood live; yea, I said unto thee: In thy blood live" (Ezekiel 16:6). The first phrase is understood by those at the *brit* as a reference to the blood of the circumcision, the second phrase as a reference to the blood that marked the doorways before the Exodus. In the thirteenth century, the cloth the circumciser used to wipe his blood-stained hands and mouth was hung at the door of the synagogue as a sign of God's protection, to recall the blood that marked the doorways of the Israelites in Exodus, and men prayed, studied, and watched the child during the night before the circumcision, *Wachnacht,* in order to ensure divine protection from evil spirits.[4]

The Torah presents both circumcision and eating unleavened bread at Passover as public, crucial statements of social inclusion as well as times of reaffirmation of the covenant. In each case, failure to act carries the penalty of being cut off from the community: "An uncircumcised male who does not circumcise the flesh of his foreskin—such a person shall be cut off from his kin" (Genesis 17:14). "Seven days you shall eat unleavened bread . . . for whoever eats leavened bread from the first day to the seventh day, that person shall be cut off from Israel" (Exodus 12:15, 19).

The relation of children to redemption, the *brit,* and Passover is also found in the Book of Joshua, which continues the story of the passage into the Promised Land after the death of Moses. The children of the freed slaves cross into the Promised Land; their fathers, who were often disobedient, were made to wander the desert until they died. As at the Red Sea, the waters of the Jordan River roll back before the children of Israel as they accompany the priests carrying the Ark of the Torah across the dry river bed. "Children" is used in the Book of Joshua

4. The protective nature of the association with Exodus is seen in the medieval use of Exodus 6:6–7, which lists God's four promises of redemption, as a formula to counteract danger.

in the same sense as at the Seder, to describe both the descendants and the collective membership of Israel. The first act of Joshua on reaching the Promised Land is to circumcise the uncircumcised males who had been raised in the wilderness. The celebration of the Passover follows this declaration of the covenant (Joshua 5:2–11).

Protected, hopeful transition, suggested by the child and Elijah, the leader's white robe and the plate of eggs, is underlined by the popular conception of Elijah as wandering the earth dressed in the desert clothes of a bedouin or the nondescript clothing of a beggar. In addition, the specially guarded *shmurah* matzah suggests both the vulnerability of the assembled people and their awareness of being in a state between slavery and freedom, as well as in a protected state.

The circular shape of this metaphoric representation of man is a form used throughout the culture to express a protection from demons, that is, from disorder and darkness. In the words of a fifteenth-century scholar, Menahem Ziyuni, "Those who invoke demons draw circles around themselves because the spirits have not the power to trespass from the public to a private area" (Trachtenberg 1974:121), and so the magician who planned to invoke the spirits first drew a circle around himself. In the Middle Ages, circles were drawn about any person considered to be in a vulnerable state, such as a woman after childbirth or a dying man. Especially protective are seven circles or three circles: the bride's circuits around the groom, the seven processions around the synagogue, and the three circles made over the head with a fowl during the scapegoat ceremony of *kapparah* on the eve of Yom Kippur.[5] At the end of the *shivah* period following a death, mourners make three walks, or circles, around the house. At the Seder, the child draws a circle of purity around all the celebrants as he carries the water for the ritual handwashing, and even if the water is passed from one to the other, as is occasionally done, the same pure ring is still created.

On both "new year" festivals, Rosh Hashana and Passover, bread assumes a circular shape. The festive Rosh Hashana bread is leavened but round: "like the year" is the most common explanation. At the Seder, the three unleavened "guarded" breads silently awaken the concepts implicit in "three," "circles," "whiteness," and "bread," to

5. The circles, made with a hen for a female and a cock for a male, are accompanied by biblical phrases and the words, "This is my substitute, this is my surrogate, this is my atonement." The fowl is then slaughtered. Despite the fact that the Code of Jewish Law discourages the rite as a "silly custom," *kapparah* has persisted among the more traditional groups. Today, instead of a fowl, the circles may be made with coins and some of the coins then donated to charity.

represent the purity, awareness of danger, and the still guarded state of the men at the table.

All the concepts of child, transition, and redemption come together in the simple game of stealing the *afikoman*. The *afikoman* is taken from the middle of the three matzahs covered with a cloth. The matzahs are arranged in a hierarchy representing the ancient caste structure of Israel, which is still recalled each time a child is named as well as during synagogue ritual. The castes are emphasized by the folds of the napkin that separate the matzahs, their unity by their inclusion under one fine cloth. The upper matzah is called the "*kohen*" (from the line of High Priests); the middle, the "Levi" (the general priestly caste); and the lower, the "Israel" (the rest of the population, as well, of course, as the name for the collective).

It is through the matzahs that the concept of incompletion that pervades the Seder is suggested again and again. The perfection and wholeness of the cups, dishes, clothes, and house attests to the goal of the evening, a state of social perfection and oneness with God. Almost immediately after the ceremony has begun, however, the middle of the three whole matzahs is broken, and part of it is taken from the table to be used as the *afikoman*. Now only two and a half breads remain to be used by the celebrants for the two benedictions over the bread and the raising of the matzah during the recitation of *HaLachma Anya*. The two and a half, incomplete loaves of matzah are consistent with the words "Lo, this is the bread of affliction," and underscore the unfulfilled, desert state of the evening. Similarly, during the second benediction, the one particular to the Seder and to matzah, when only the upper one and a half matzahs are raised, the afflicted state is once again made apparent.

However, a problem arises during the first benediction, the one said at all festivals. It is a problem of use and interpretation that affects the comprehension of the evening as imbued more heavily with either hope or despair. Throughout the year, two whole loaves of bread must be present at a festival, to indicate the double joy of the time. There is disagreement on whether the leader should raise just the upper two—actually one and a half—matzahs at this time, or whether, because they are incomplete, all three matzahs should be raised. Some sources (the Code of Jewish Law and Kahn, in particular) insist on raising just the upper one and a half matzahs, as they insist on the use of the *kittel*, the plate of eggs, and tasting the full bitterness of the herbs by making the *haroset* very liquid and shaking it off the herbs before they are eaten.

Others, like Roth, reject the negative implications present in raising less than two whole loaves for the benediction and would have all three matzahs raised as an affirmation of the joyousness of the festival.

The upper *kohen* and Levi "priestly" matzahs are distributed to be eaten with the mixture of sweet and bitter, *haroset* and bitter herbs. The Israel "ordinary people" matzah encloses the bitter herbs alone before it is eaten, expressing and making personal the relation of the collective people of Israel and the experience of bitterness.

At the start of the last part of the Seder, which focuses on redemption, only the *afikoman* portion of the Levi matzah remains. In the Bible, Levi is the landless priestly tribe to which Moses belongs. The tribe is to be landless because, as priests, their primary loyalty must be to the atemporal deity and their primary function is to officiate at his altars, no matter where in the land they may be found. Moses epitomizes the intermediary position of his landless tribe: although he communicates most directly with God, he never completes the historical process of reaching the Promised Land. At the Seder, if only one piece of *shmurah* matzah is available, it must be used for the Levi matzah, and thus the concept of being specially guarded is even more closely identified with the landless priestly tribe.

The setting aside of the *afikoman* sums up the experience of the people of the diaspora. Levi (the priestly people) is broken (dispersed) and exiled from the table (Altar, Temple, Jerusalem) to be returned (redeemed) by the children (messiahs). The larger portion of Levi has been exiled; only a small portion has remained by the Altar in Jerusalem.

Often some of the returned *afikoman* is not eaten but kept until the following year in the pages of the Haggadah. Hidden this way, this last food of the Seder extends the experiences of the Seder throughout the year. As this bit of *afikoman* lingers in exile, it acts as a metaphor for the experience of *galut.*

Many folk beliefs have clustered about the *afikoman* to explain why it is not totally consumed. The *afikoman* has been seen as a charm, to bring good luck in the year to come and prolong life. "He ate too much *afikoman*" is said of a person who dies very old. A piece of *afikoman* preserved during the year is also interpreted to mean that no matter how poor the family, it will not be without food. In this belief the ideas of food and bread as a gift of the divine meet in man's version of the bread of the desert.

In Sephardic custom, a conscious connection is made between the *afikoman* and the period of desert wanderings. At Seders in the Mediterranean tradition, the *afikoman* is not stolen or hidden away. Instead, it is wrapped in a napkin and placed on the shoulder, as a "pack on the back while traveling to Jerusalem," and the bundle is transferred from one to another until all have had a turn carrying it. Usually it is the youngest child who first receives the *afikoman,* accepting it with the words from Exodus 12:34: "The children of Israel took their dough before it was leavened, with kneading troughs bound up in their clothes upon their shoulders." The leader then asks the child, "From where have you come?" and the child answers, "From Egypt." The next question is, "Where are you going?" and the response is, "To Jerusalem." Then the leader asks, "What provisions do you have for the way?" and the child answers by pointing to the matzah he carries.

That the passage through the desert is under God's protection, and that the Seder is evocative of even greater proximity to God, is expressed through the use of the *afikoman* in Morocco as a charm against misfortune while traveling, and in other eastern lands as a charm to ward off the evil eye.

The relation of children to promises of joy is expressed not only through their carrying the *afikoman* but also through the full cups of wine that stand before the participants during each passage in the Seder dealing specifically with children. In the Seder, a quite conscious connection is made between full wine cups and joy and empty ones and the absence of joy. The emptying of the wine cups during the reading of the Ten Plagues is commonly explained as an expression of diminished joy because of the sufferings of the Egyptians. More subtly, the deliberate timing of the pouring, raising, and drinking of the wine causes the cups to be empty whenever the matzah is uncovered and raised and the afflicted state recalled. Whenever the cups are filled and raised, the matzah is hidden.

The cups are empty during the reading of "Lo, this is the bread of affliction," but the matzah is covered and the cups are filled before the next passage, the child's asking of the Four Questions. They are also full during the section concerning the Four Sons. The four cups of wine are themselves justified by the Talmud as relating to the four promises of redemption used by God in Exodus [6:6–7]. "Four" may be dared tonight as an affirmation of God's protective watch. Still, if odd numbers are less dangerous than even ones, three sets of four are safer still. Although the use of three sets of four may have originated in the protective properties of certain numbers, at the Seder "four," united through the auspicious "three," joins children, joy, and redemption.

When the children return the *afikoman* at the very beginning of the final section of the Seder, the focus for redemption shifts from the child to Elijah. By this point the assembly has demonstrated its compliance with the laws, praised God, and been united like children in pure community once again to learn and accept the divine history. As at the end of the purificatory Days of Atonement, which place them in a state suitable for moral return, the participants are in a perfected state suitable for seeing the end of the historical process they have been recounting. Both periods of purification end with the words "Next year in Jerusalem!" To this end, they fill the cup with wine and open the door for Elijah.

There is a legend that "when Elijah comes, all unsolved questions will be answered." The question of the necessary cups of wine at the Seder, either for protective purposes or because of a questionable fifth reference to redemption in the Book of Exodus, is said to be solved by connecting the extra, fifth cup of wine with the prophet. This aspect of Elijah as a problem solver, like his role as the herald of the messiah, makes Elijah the personification of completion, *shalom.* The positioning and handling of the cup for Elijah—finally filled near the end of the Seder—complements the meanings attached to him.

God's messenger is believed to wander from town to town to bring hope in times of distress.[6] As he goes from community to community, he becomes aware of the hospitality and righteousness of the people, and whether or not they are worthy of the messiah. Elijah thus represents the most positive and negative poles of Jewish existence. Dressed as a bedouin, wandering the earth, he is placed at a distance from his God but is in immediate communication with him. He suggests hope and joy by acknowledging distress; he lives among the temporal but exists in the eternal; and he suggests future synthesis while testifying to the present disparities between the promise and the actual. The door is opened for Elijah only after the participants have complied with the direction to tell the story of the Passover and eat the matzah, and after

6. The wanderer Elijah shares a relationship with other liminal figures, the "threshold or edge men" (Turner 1968:580). "Elijah" might be substituted for Eshu in Joan Wescott's description of the Yoruba trickster Eshu-Elegba: "[Eshu] is . . . described as a homeless wandering spirit, and as one who inhabits the marketplace, the crossroads, and the thresholds of houses. He is present whenever there is change and transition" (1962: 337). However, Elijah is not a classical trickster in that he exhibits no self-will, caprice, or ambiguous sexual status. Like all prophets in Hebrew lore, he is always directed by God.

they have demonstrated their acceptance of God's law and their appreciation for the Exodus. When they formally open the door to welcome the prophet, Elijah's absence is suggested: no similar ceremony "welcomes" Elijah at the *brit* or *Havdalah;* at these times his presence as part of the community is assumed. The emphatic invitation and the prominent position of Elijah's cup speak of the importance of present deliverance to the Seder.

Opening the door appears to be a ritual imperative made rational by the understanding that Elijah might enter.[7] Although the opening of the door is mandated by the Haggadah, Elijah's name is not mentioned at this time. As a relatively late addition to the Passover ceremony, "the opening of the door" is especially expressive of the *galut* experience that created it.

Opening the door for Elijah has a lovely air of living a legend, but it makes no sense in terms of the considerations for safety of those who developed the Seder. Starting in the twelfth century, a succession of massacres took place on Passover. The Seder was disturbed on numerous occasions throughout Europe by armed mobs who believed the "blood accusations"—rumors that Jews used Christian blood in the manufacture of the matzah and as wine. There are many records of celebrants being slaughtered on this evening. This would seem *not* to be the time to open the door, an invitation to disaster, and yet the custom persisted. It has been explained as a way of demonstrating to the Christian populace that no blood was in fact being used, and as a mark of hospitality. Yet, as a sign of hospitality, opening the door is an empty gesture, since at this point all the food has been eaten and only one more cup of wine may be drunk.

One of the main concerns of the evening has been the building of the sense of community, a closed community, as represented by the protective circle around the table. To open the door—the boundary of this closed world—would seem to break this circle unless, in fact, it *extends* the circle to other homes where the doors are also being opened. Opening the door is a concrete action aimed at the realization of the extended community to which the Seder refers through language and symbol. Elijah wanders from community to community, from open door to open door. As he sips wine in each home, he not only brings communication from town to town in the *galut,* but from God to man.

7. In many communities, opening the door is the occasion for an informal drama. One of the participants might hide outside and step into the house as Elijah when the door is opened, to the delight of the children.

Through the medium of Elijah and the open door, the Jew shares the Passover Seder with all other Jews who are celebrating the festival throughout the world on the same evening. And because the eternal Elijah has been present at Seders in days past and will drink the wine at future celebrations, he connects the present participants to communities past and future.

The door is opened with the words:

> Pour out thy wrath upon the nations that know Thee not, and upon the kingdoms that call not upon Thy name. For they have devoured Jacob, and laid waste his land. Pour out Thy indignation upon them, and let the fierceness of Thy anger overtake them. Pursue them in anger, and destroy them from under the heavens of the Lord.

These words, from Psalms and Lamentations, are the only ones specifically calling for harm to present-day oppressors. Even the recitation of the Ten Plagues is qualified by the explanation given for the spilling of the wine.

In the first part of the Haggadah, God's might and anger are praised as necessary and instrumental in deliverance. In this last section, God's might and anger are supplicated, even demanded, in order to achieve redemption for the present population. The Hebrew words are both an urgent address to God and a means of protection as the door is opened for this necessary, but dangerous, ceremony. The words on the opening of the door attest to the desire for the warrior as well as for the gentle messiah.

In America, the words are sometimes dropped, and a simple song welcoming Elijah *(Eliahu HaNavi)* is substituted. This substitution indicates a perception of non-Jewish society as nonthreatening, "non-devouring." By de-emphasizing anger and suffering, the promise of the covenant is made to appear less urgent.

The thematic transition in the Seder from child to Elijah carries with it the concept of hope as inherent in change. It is especially through the "child" that transition becomes promise, not just ambiguity or danger. If, as the Talmud says, "Jerusalem was destroyed only because the children did not attend school, and loitered in the streets" (Sabbath 119b), then the Seder exhibits the creation of a new Jerusalem as the child comes in from the streets and asks questions, and as all the participants, like children, relearn the story. Like another symbol of transition, the *kittel*, the child is "white" and not gray, a statement of an ideal future and not an indeterminate present.

8
The Summarizing Plate

> When the Israelites do God's will, they make His left hand as His right hand; but when they do not do His will, they make, if one may say so, His right hand as His left.
>
> *The Midrash*

The circular Seder plate echoes the enclosing circle of the people grouped around the table, the circle made by the children carrying water, the *shmurah* matzah, and the perfect wine cups and dinner plates. The plate is often referred to as "the table," and stands in metonymical relationship to the Seder table. It sums up and "protects" the ideas presented during the evening.

In addition to the matzah and the wine, it is on the Seder plate that the Seder's quintessential concepts exist in tangible form. Items are raised, dipped, combined, eaten, or pointed out. The plate itself is customarily removed from the table during the recitation of *HaLachma Anya* and the raising of the matzahs. If, as in some communities, the matzahs are on the same tray, the egg and bone are removed during the reading. Together the matzah and the plate are reminiscent of what Turner has termed the "sacra" at a liminal rite: familiar items of the culture presented in unfamiliar ways to provoke interest and make neophytes question and reflect upon society's truths (1970:102). The bread of ordinary days takes an unfamiliar form at the Seder, and its mysterious quality is emphasized by hiding it under a cloth throughout the ceremony. The Code of Jewish Law decrees that even when it is raised, the matzah should be uncovered only slightly.[1] The *afikoman*

1. It is customary to cover bread before the benediction at a festival meal, but to uncover it thereafter.

"disappears" through most of the ritual, and the plate "disappears" during the *HaLachma Anya*. These movements make ordinary eggs, bones, lettuce, and apples extraordinary, and focus attention on the messages they carry. The plate is returned just before the Four Questions are asked by the child. As "child" is a symbolic category, so the questions themselves are indicative of the questioning of all the evening's special items and proceedings.

Like the sacra of a rite of transition, the plate is "the heart of the liminal matter" (Turner 1970:102). The bounded circle of the Seder plate provides the most extreme, inclusive focusing of the ideas implicit in the culture and contemplated at the ritual. "Children," new and old, "are alternately forced and encouraged to think about their society" (Turner 1970:105) by having the constructs of the society laid before them. These constructs are suggested by materials common to daily life but gathered or prepared just for the Seder, and arranged on the plate in a manner consistent with the structuring of ideas and relationships throughout the year.

In the Haggadah there are precise instructions for the placement and movement of persons and items. All must recline to the left to drink the wine but sit upright when eating the matzah and bitter herbs. The items are put on the Seder plate in a specific manner; the bone and egg are neither raised nor lowered, but the bitter herbs may be both raised and lowered. Rather than isolated instructions for an evening's ceremony, such directional imperatives are consistent with actions throughout the year. It matters that one reclines to the left not only because such movement frees the more frequently used hand, but because the general symbolism carried by concepts such as "left" and "right" supports the more specific meanings of the Seder.

"Right" implies "good," "positive," "dominant," "sacred." It is God's "right hand" that is powerful:

> Your right hand, O Lord, glorious in power,
> Your right hand, O Lord, shatters the foe! [Exodus 15:6]

The right hand is clever:

> If I forget thee, O Jerusalem,
> Let my right hand forget her cunning. [Psalm 137:5–6]

The right hand is tender:

> In dealing with a child and a woman, the left hand should repel and the right hand should caress. [Code of Jewish Law, vol. 4, 165:7]

When they are being consecrated to God as priests, Aaron and his sons are touched with the blood of sacrifice on the right side of the body.

In daily life, things to be honored are placed on the right. The *Kiddush* cup of festival wine is raised in the right hand, the *mezuzah* is hung on the right side of the doorway, and Elijah sits at the right of the *sandek,* the man who holds the child at the *brit.* Circular movements within the synagogue, including processions with the Torah, enclose the congregation from right to left. During Hannukah, candles are put into the candelabrum, or *hannukiah,* from right to left, and are lit from left to right.[2] In this way, the candles on the right are the last to be extinguished.

The Code of Jewish Law decrees that when dressing one must "give precedence to the right hand or foot over the left; but when removing shoes and other articles of apparel the left hand comes first" (vol. 1, 3:4). The right hand is cleansed first in ritual washing, and the right hand places the black *tefillin* on the head and left arm.

"Left" stands in opposition to "right" to connote evil and sadness. A mourner tears his clothes (or, today, wears a black button) on the left for parents, on the right for other close kin. The evil inclination is said by the Hasidim to reside in the left side of the heart, and to whisper in the left ear; the good *yetzer* is in the right ventricle of the heart and whispers in the right ear.[3] Folklore has many practices consistent with the good-evil representations of right and left: to thwart the evil eye, one looks down the left side of his nose, itching of the left eye indicates tears, of the right, joy; and salt thrown over the left shoulder of the bride and groom protects them against demons.

Left is associated with north, also a negative direction. This connection can be seen in the orientation of the marriage ceremony. At a wedding, whether before the Torah in the synagogue or under the stars in the synagogue courtyard, the couple faces east, the bride to the right and south, the groom to the left and north. Similarly, at the Seder, when the plate is placed before the leader on the table, the top is toward the east, the right side, with the bone and *haroset,* is toward the south, and the left side, with the egg and greens, is toward the north.

In Leviticus, the power of the left is countered by placing the protective sign of the priestly covenant, salt, on the north side of the altar. According to the folklore of the Middle Ages, demons approach

2. Hannukah commemorates the victory of the Jews over the ancient Syrians. Candles are lit each night for eight days, an additional one each night. This practice is said to recall the small amount of oil found in the Temple, apparently only enough for one day, which burned for eight.

3. Schneur Zalman of Liadi (1972:99).

from the north. The bridegroom standing on the left would fight the jealous demons by throwing the emptied wine glass against the north wall. Lauterbach thinks that this is the origin of the modern custom of breaking a glass at a wedding, a custom that has been given new meaning (1970:19). Today the breaking of the glass is commonly explained as a reminder that the Temple is still in a state of destruction, like the glass, and that even at the happy time of a wedding, the community's joy remains incomplete. However, after the groom steps on the glass at the end of the ceremony, the wedding guests all cry out, "Mazel tov!" or "Good luck!"

The "mixed nature" of the female as potential for both good and evil is shown through the symbolism of "right" and "left." The woman indicates her natural association with the sacred by standing to the right of the groom at the wedding, and the socially honored state of marriage is recognized by placing the ring on the right hand. Yet in the Zohar the female is consistently associated with darkness, north, and "left" in opposition to the male's "right." This "left" nature of the female, whether the woman or the idealized Community of Israel in relation with God, can be explained through the concept of subordination, which is also part of the web of meanings expressed through the simple direction "left."

"Left" and "right" as metaphoric ways of conveying negative and positive characteristics are not tied to a physical base. In insisting that the left hand be used to clean oneself after the toilet, the Code of Jewish Law uses "left" to connote impurity, but when it remarks, "A left-handed person should clean himself with the right hand, which is like everyone else's left hand" (vol. 1, 4:5), "left" suggests "subordination." If one's left hand is strong, it is "right": "A fully left-handed man . . . must put on *tefillah* ["prayer," that is, the phylactery] on the right hand which is equivalent to everyone's left" (vol. 1, 10:12). Therefore, a left-handed person making *Kiddush* holds the wine cup in the left hand. During penitential prayers *(Tahanun)* worshipers place their heads on their left arms and silently confess their sins. This rite is considered a "falling on the face," or ritual prostration, and echoes the prostration of the pious during Yom Kippur prayers. In this practice the meanings of "left" and "down," as subordination, deference, or impurity, meet and contrast with the positive messages carried by "right" and "up." Moses ascended a mountain to receive the Torah, and one still "ascends" to read the Torah, go to Jerusalem, and emigrate to Israel *(aliyah,* "ascending"). The Torah is raised before being returned to the Ark with the eternal light shining above it, one rises to greet Elijah, and in ritual purification the body is lowered to remove impurity and raised into a pure state. Conversely, one "goes down" *(yiridah)* when leaving Jerusalem or Israel, and at a funeral the mourner sits on low benches and the body might be placed on the floor before being buried.

The meanings of "up" and "down," "right" and "left" come together at the *bimah,* the platform on which the Torah is read. It is valid to approach the Torah from either right or left, for one is thought to be so eager to reach the Torah that direction is not important. However, it can be seen that there is no right or left in the Torah itself, for in winding the scroll left continuously becomes right.[4] This synthesis through the Law, which makes right or left irrelevant, extends to the area around the Torah. The raised platform stands as a symbol, in exile, of the Temple.

When, therefore, the Haggadah instructs the participants to raise the wine glasses, or raise the "bread of affliction," it is doing more than merely enabling the items to be displayed to the group (which has in any case seen them many times already). It is making a statement about the ideas being activated by the material forms. Similarly, the location of the items on the Seder plate is indicative of the concepts they carry.

The plate falls easily into a "nature/culture" dichotomy. The upper symbols, which represent "culture," are transformed animal or vegetable forms; the lower items are in their natural state. The bitter herbs in the center participate in and mediate all poles.

MATZAHS

Although Rabbi Luria's arrangement places the matzahs at the top center of the plate, more frequently they are on a plate of their own. Still, in the traditional arrangement the top center remains the position of the matzahs. This placement combines "left" and "right," affliction and election, but is more positive than negative because it is at the top, "up." The position supports the meanings of the matzah as the most perfected expression of Jewish society, the "bread of affliction" that is honored, raised, because affliction through election is part of the divine plan.

BONE

The roasted bone, with its meat, occupies the most favored position on the plate, the upper right. The bone is hard, white, whole, and durable. Like the egg, the bone is neither raised nor lowered through-

4. Hebrew is read from right to left.

out the ritual. Although the bone is described as a "shankbone," in practice any bone with meat is acceptable. Because poultry is the most common main course at the meal in America, the bone is often a chicken or turkey bone. In the Middle East, it may be a lamb bone. The Haggadah describes the bone as the symbol of the ancient Paschal sacrifice and the sacrifices to come when the Temple is restored. The

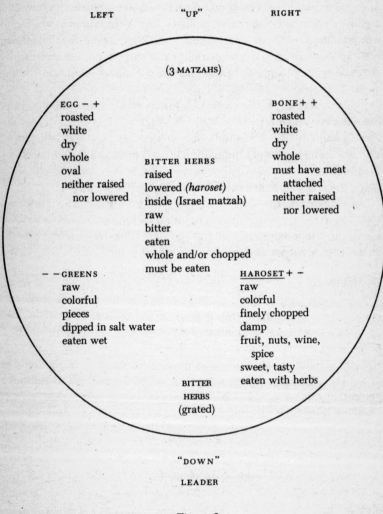

LEFT   "UP"   RIGHT

(3 MATZAHS)

EGG − +
roasted
white
dry
whole
oval
neither raised
    nor lowered

BITTER HERBS
raised
lowered *(haroset)*
inside (Israel matzah)
raw
bitter
eaten
whole and/or chopped
must be eaten

BONE + +
roasted
white
dry
whole
must have meat
    attached
neither raised
    nor lowered

− −GREENS
raw
colorful
pieces
dipped in salt water
eaten wet

HAROSET + −
raw
colorful
finely chopped
damp
fruit, nuts, wine,
    spice
sweet, tasty
eaten with herbs

BITTER
HERBS
(grated)

"DOWN"

LEADER

Figure 3.
The Seder plate.

ancient sacrifice was a first-born male lamb or goat, but all first-born males, animals or human, were consecrated to God. Today, first-born males are still redeemed from service at the *Pidyon HaBen,* and the entire people of Israel is still called the first-born of God. The one idea of consecration carried by the bone subsumes the ideas of animal, male Jew, and nation of Israel.

The name of the bone, "forearm" *(zero'a),* is compatible with the upper right placement of the bone and the metaphoric identity of the Paschal sacrifice with the nation of Israel. The usual explanation of the name is that it refers to God's forearm, which brought the Israelites from Egypt. However, when joined to the concept of a consecrated first-born, a "light unto all nations," Israel is the sacred and powerful "forearm" of God on earth. It is the meat on the bone that marks the symbol as specifically male, since to be present at the table males and meat undergo parallel cultural transformations. At the same time, the "male" bone includes the female, as "mankind" includes both men and women. "Woman" is created from "man" in Genesis, and in Judaism is still part of man. Each is dependent on the other for fulfilling the obligations of the culture and cannot stand alone.

The bone, then, summarizes the ideas of Jewish culture dedicated to God, through males. Its upper right, very "positive" placement expresses the strength and sacred honor of the relationship, as does its white color. As everlasting "culture" it is a cold, cooked, durable form, a message also carried by the matzah and the egg.

Although both the bone and the matzah express the relation of a consecrated culture to its god, it is the matzah that is the touchstone of the holiday and the *afikoman* that is said to take the place of the Paschal sacrifice. The matzah is commemorative but also representative of the current state of exile; the bone is commemorative and promissory of the ideal state of the Temple.

This shift of symbols is consistent with the transfer of the celebration of the Exodus from among the throngs in the Temple courtyard to the intimacy and enclosure of the home.[5] The central symbol of the Passover celebration, the sacrifice cooked outside over an open fire, has been replaced by a food baked inside a doubly enclosed space, an oven either in the home or in a communal bakery. The key Passover food has been changed from an event of the evening, a sacrificial meal, to a form

5. Josephus estimates that there were three million Jews gathered in Jerusalem in 65 C.E. for the last Passover before the Temple was destroyed (*Encyclopedia Judaica Jerusalem,* 13:163).

whose production brings the community together and focuses its collective mind for weeks before the festival. Matzah is also used to extend the community: the absolute need of each Jew to have matzah for the holidays has resulted in annual collections of money to buy matzah for the needy and mailings of matzah where none can be baked, to men in the armed services, for example, or to the Soviet Union today.

In addition to losing its place as the central symbol, meat cooked like the sacrifice in direct contact with fire—barbecued or broiled—has been prohibited as a main dish for the festival meal. "Baked" meats, meats cooked in an oven, or in a receptacle, are permitted, and oven-roasted lamb, fowl, or beef is a common main course. While the change dismisses the possibility of a virtual re-enactment of the ancient sacrifice, it also makes a statement about the relationship of the community to God. The meat of sacrifice is in an unmediated state of direct contact with fire. Therefore, sacrifice is a vehicle of communication between mankind and God, because consuming fire suggests an immediate relationship with the Divine. This is the sense of the burning of the *hallah* portion of the bread. The substitution of meat warmed slowly and indirectly through a receptacle is compatible with the distant-but-present relationship, as in the desert, between God and man in *galut.* [6]

The shift from food and symbol transformed by immediate contact with fire to one more distant from the source of heat and light parallels Lévi-Strauss's distinction between exo-cuisine and endo-cuisine, food cooked outside the house over a fire, and that prepared inside the home. Such inside forms are termed "boiled," but "boiled" here denotes the state of containment inside a receptacle, possibly but not necessarily immersion in a liquid. In this sense, food prepared in an oven is "boiled," endo-cuisine. Exo-cuisine is food generally shared with guests; endo-cuisine is family food: beef stew and not barbecued beef. The Paschal sacrifice was specifically a form of exo-cuisine: "Do not eat

6. The English custom of having fish as the main meal (Roth 1959:44) avoids any semblance of re-enactment of the sacrifice, but it is consistent with the transitional spring setting of the Seder. Jewish legend connects fish with purity because of their home in the water and because the ever open eyes of the fish are said to be reminiscent of the watchfulness of God. Whatever the reason, the *Tashlikh* ceremony of purification is ideally observed at a stream with fish in it, and among Sephardic Jews, many of whom settled in England, fish is often the main dish on Rosh Hashana. The centerpiece on the table at the Moroccan ceremony of Mimouna, which concludes the Passover week, is a whole fish. It cannot be determined here, by these few examples, whether associations such as these have influenced the English practice, but serving fish agrees with the meanings that cluster at the Seder.

any of it raw, or cooked in any way with water, but roasted—head, legs, and entrails—over the fire" (Exodus 12:9). Matzah and the meats of the meal are inside, "boiled" forms, prepared within a cultural receptacle, within a culturally defined, bounded home, according to strict rules. Although the Paschal sacrifice, like the matzah of the Seder, was eaten in family groups, the change of symbolic form of the central food of the Passover ritual perhaps reflects not only physical problems in continuing the sacrifice among nonpastoral populations, but even more the changed social circumstances of the celebrants.

The Passover meal has always been a proclamation of the distinction between "insiders" and "outsiders." What has changed through time is the degree to which the concept of "insider" could be extended to include the society immediately surrounding the family group. The sacrifice in Egypt is the first public declaration by the slaves of their distinctive identity through their relationship to God, and this solidifies the group prior to the Exodus. It is a statement through which the members might recognize each other and openly acknowledge their unity. In Israel also, the public sacrifice at the Temple centered on family units, but the distinction between family and immediate society was not as great as it was later to become in the diaspora. Then the public celebration declared national unity, both within the society and in relation to God, and reinforced the distinctiveness of the nation of Israel as opposed to the surrounding populations, a distinction repeatedly commanded by God in the Torah.

In the diaspora, the extended society was no longer an extension of the family. Even where Jews lived in relatively circumscribed communities, the loss of their land and national state, the sense of difference from the surrounding populations, and the perception of isolation from other Jewish settlements and from God, all contributed to the transformation of "nation" into the more narrowed and specialized concept of "community" as an extended kinship relation. The ritual was moved into the home, behind closed doors, reflecting both the tightened definition of family and community and the security considerations of the times. The opening of the door toward the end of the Seder still signals the relationship of isolated family groups with the whole community and with God, but that relationship is lifted from one of immediate, physical proximity, as at the Temple, to the more abstract and encompassing relationship across time and space, expressed through the figure of Elijah, the eternal communicator between the society and God, and between separated populations. The boiled forms of the Seder—the matzah, the baked meat, and the baked egg—reinforce this tightened definition of community.

The matzah, then, as carrier of the message of the diaspora, is featured at the Seder much more prominently than the bone. The bone is given a place of honor and pointed out, but it is removed from the table when the matzah is raised. Leaving the bone on the table would reinforce the matzah's message of priestliness and hope. Removing the bone allows the message of affliction to be heard more clearly.

EGG

The other "culture" symbol is the roasted (baked) egg on the upper left of the plate. Although a necessary component of the Seder plate, the egg is not explained in the Haggadah narrative as are the bone, herbs, and matzah. It is commonly understood to represent the additional sacrifices brought to the Temple on the festivals of Passover, Shavuot, and Sukkot. These sacrifices were not, in any case, eggs.

The egg, like the *kittel*, supports the transitional symbolism of the Seder. In its immediate association as the only food necessary at a funeral, the egg points to death and mourning. Another common explanation for the egg—that it is a token of grief for the fallen Temple—acknowledges this association. Still, the whiteness of the egg and the *kittel* suggests the sacred and hence the presence of the eternal in animal forms and in man's nature, hope as well as despair. The egg is "new life," made cultural and lasting through cooking, and consecrated through browning or singeing—obvious contact with fire. Its endless oval shape is used to convey the idea of life everlasting. Once these ideas are established, an actual egg is unimportant to the ceremony. A white, boiled potato on the upper left carries the same meaning. The death-to-life contradiction in the egg is carried in its negative (left) and positive (upper) placement, and is compatible with the winter-to-spring season of Passover and the Seder's concern with the passage from Egypt to Jerusalem.

The "positive side" of the egg is expressed in folklore, which says that anyone lucky enough to secure the egg from the plate after the two Seders will be assured of good fortune, and any wish he expresses will be fulfilled. At the Seder in the eastern European tradition, the entire community is given the possibility of good fortune through the additional plate of eggs. Although these eggs recall the many eggs at a funeral meal, at the Seder they become instruments of hope. Each individual dips an egg into salt water before the meal begins.

This "purificatory bath" reinforces the positive connotations of the egg.

In formally stressing the positive pole of the egg's meanings, the Seder acknowledges the power of the negative; its optimistic message is carried in a manner reminiscent of a funeral. The eggs counteract the danger to the community much as the mnemonic words negate the meanings of the Ten Plagues. The introduction of this extra measure of active hope, the "good luck charm," is itself a recognition of distress.

Nature's symbols occupy the lower half of the Seder plate.

GREENS

The greens, on the lower left, have the least favored position. They are raw, unelaborated, dry, tasty, and colorful. The lettuce, parsley, or celery (or any other fresh green) represents vegetation, nature that grows and decays each year. Raw onions and potatoes, which are sometimes substituted for the lettuce or parsley, are both vegetables that produce green shoots.

The only other use of vegetation in Jewish ritual is at the fall festival of Sukkot, where the association is with the temporary dwellings of the wilderness and the *Hoshana* prayers for salvation. When related to the greens of Sukkot, the greens of Passover are suggestive of transitional periods of nature and specifically of the spring season of nature's re-awakening. The greens, like the egg, thus support themes of the Seder.

Vegetation is accorded its recognition and dispensed with early in the Seder by its "purification" through immersion in the bath of salt water. It is the least important element in the story of the evening, as its negative placement suggests. Those symbols still on the plate all have more importance to the story than the greens.

HAROSET

The *haroset* ("clay") on the lower right is usually a finely chopped mixture of apples, nuts, raisins, cinnamon, and wine. It is reddish brown, tasty, sweet, and moist. Ingredients vary widely according to locale, but *haroset* always contains fruits, spices, and with rare exceptions, a fermented liquid. The *haroset* is neither raised nor lowered, and it is not explained in the Haggadah, although it is commonly understood to represent the mortar used by the Israelites in Egypt. The bitter herbs are dipped in it, or it is eaten with the herbs between the Levi matzah. The fourteenth-century legal compilation, the *Tur,* specifically connects *haroset* with spring because of the fruit and nuts (*Tur,* chap. 473, Abudarham), and apples and other fruits are associated with the observance of the fall New Year celebration of Rosh Hashana. Apples dipped in honey begin the meal at Rosh Hashana, new fruits of the season may be blessed and eaten, and foods containing apples and other fruits are often served.

The *haroset,* placed on the right like the woman at the wedding, is a female symbol. Its ingredients—culturally defined but inherently unstable materials of fruit and fermenting liquid—share the female's compromised status between "nature" and "culture." Its main ingredients suggest "life": fruit and nuts indicate new life, but with the decaying wine, the impermanence of life also. Wine also contributes the idea of joy. This idea of the joy of transitory life is carried in the custom of giving nuts to children on Passover.

Throughout biblical literature, women are allied with life-bearing fruit, starting with Eve, whose name in Hebrew means "life." Psalm 128:3 compares a woman to a "fruitful vine," and the lines in the Song of Songs: "Under the apple-tree I awakened thee; / There thy mother was in travail with thee; / There was she in travail and brought thee forth" (8:5), are said to refer to a legend that when Pharaoh decreed death to all Hebrew children, the women gave birth in the apple orchards and the children were raised by angels (Roth 1959:ix). As with the egg, the woman's association with life and death is supported by the *haroset*'s positive (right) and negative (lower) placement.

The moistness of the *haroset* also suggests the female, through her associations with blood and the waters of ritual immersion. The normally pasty *haroset* is made even more liquid when it is thinned with wine to ensure that it does not adhere to the bitter herbs. And wine's role as a medium of social and divine connection is enhanced by the addition of spices, which are used in Jewish ritual to express the sweet smell of the sacred. At *Havdalah* at the end of each Sabbath a spice box is passed around for everyone to smell while the candle burns. This practice, said to "extend the sweetness of the Sabbath into the weekdays to come," is reminiscent of the burning of incense at the Temple altar, and the sweet-smelling flowers at the Seder. In ancient times, spices were put into the water with which the dead were washed and into the coffin.

That aspect of the woman's relationship with nature which circumvents the control of the male and the Law is also expressed through the association of the female with fruit. It is Eve, the female, who takes the first bite of the fruit of the tree of knowledge and induces Adam to eat it. The fruit, often referred to as the "apple," is the direct embodiment of God's knowledge: it confers immediate awareness of good and evil. This ability to discriminate between good and evil removes the male and female of Eden from the state of mindless bliss and causes their exile. In banishing them from Eden, God also separates them from immortality, from the possibility of eating from the tree of life (Genesis 3:6, 22).

In contrast to the female's undisciplined initiation of communication with God through the sensual fruit of knowledge, God initiates the communication through the rationalized, opaque word of the Torah and places the Law in the hands of Moses and the males. The Torah provides the Jews with a means of finding their way back to Eden, the state of bliss and unity, Jerusalem. The events of Sinai are therefore an inversion of the process of Eden, and a commentary on the character of the woman; she is shown as associated with nature in its suprahuman aspects and also as in need of social control through the agency of the male.

The woman's pathway to the divine is through amorphous, sensual means—fire, water—and her closest associations are with those only partially constrained by culture—the young; thus the separate items of the *haroset* are blended into a nondefinitive form. The Hebrew meaning of *haroset,* "clay," such as a potter might use, is, like the female, a concept implying potentiality, the creation of new form. Jewish thought has applied the term both to the woman herself—as in the section of the Talmud quoted above that describes a woman as a *golem* (an unformed substance, a piece of clay) to be molded by her maker, her husband—and to the community as a whole—as in Isaiah 45:9, "We are the clay, and Thou our potter." It is significant that both "creator" and "potter" may be expressed in Hebrew by the same word, *yotser.* And, as we have seen, the community has been characterized as female in its relationship with God.

As a consequence of cultural definitions, woman is potential for good and evil, the bearer of life and reminder of death, a temptress, a catalyst, who can affect man's destiny and so needs supervision and control. Because she can make her husband good or bad and cause the Shekinah to enter or depart from the home, her husband must guide her in order to ensure a positive result. Both woman and clay are molded by outside forces, but neither the Law that controls her nor the potter's creation of form changes their imprecise nature, a nature supported by the mixed, positive and negative, placement of the *haroset*.

The four symbols so far discussed thus form a series of categorical oppositions on the plate. If we allow that "up" is positive and "down" is negative, we find that culture, as represented by animal forms, is favored over nature (figure 4). This recalls Genesis 1:29–30, where God gives man dominion over everything on earth, animal and vegetable. Both items in the "culture" half of the plate are durable forms; those in the "nature" section demonstrate impermanence.

Consecrated mankind occupies the upper right, the best position, and vegetation the worst. This is not to deny the importance of vegetation in the scheme of things; vegetation would not have been accorded a position on the plate at all if it were not valued. The placement reinforces the order of importance, and underscores the enduring quality of Jewish culture as opposed to the transitory aspect of the natural world.

Another opposition can be seen on the other diagonal (figure 5). Here it is the contrast of life and death, joy and sadness, eternal and temporal life. The baked egg is life in death, the eternal preserved. The white, oval egg can suggest eternity despite the egg's deadened form.

The *haroset* represents death in life—mortality—the fermenting, rotting, decaying process even present in life-bearing forms: the eternal cycle as represented in woman.

If we look again at the plate and accept right as favored over left,

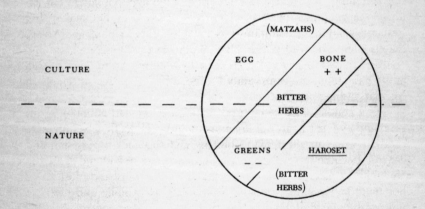

Figure 4.
The Seder plate: the social world and the natural world.

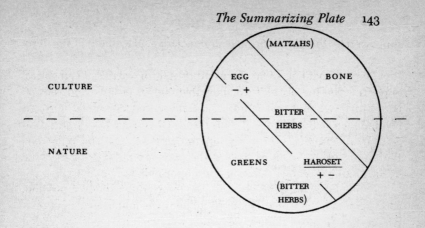

Figure 5.
The Seder plate: life and death.

we see that human life is preferred over nonhuman life (figure 6). As representative of the first-born, dedicated to God, the bone with its meat is "male" and the fruit and wine of the *haroset,* "female." They are placed on the right and are thus dominant over animal life as represented by the egg and vegetation as seen in the greens. While both man and woman are on the right side, however, man has the dominant position, the upper quadrant. This accords with the perception of roles as related in Genesis and in Jewish life.

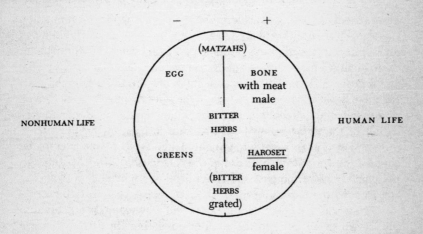

Figure 6.
The Seder plate: human and nonhuman life.

THE BITTER HERBS

In a very graphic and sensual way, the bitter herbs present a message that bitterness is part of even the most joyous of experiences. This central position, which combines right, left, up, and down, places the herbs in between all the facets of Jewish culture as expressed in the symbols of the plate—the culture, the natural world, eternal and temporal life—and makes bitterness a part of each quadrant. In addition, on plates having a second dish of herbs at the bottom, the negative component is underscored.

The placement and movement of the bitter herbs make further statements. During the narration, three symbols must be discussed because they are crucial to the meanings of the evening: "Rabban Gamaliel said: 'Whoever does not mention the meanings of the three symbols, the Paschal lamb, the unleavened bread, and the bitter herbs, has not fulfilled his obligation.'" The readings that accompany the explanation of each symbol relate explicitly to the historical time in Egypt. The bone may not be raised while being discussed, but the matzah and the bitter herbs may be raised or pointed out. When raised, the "honoring" of the herbs represents the same contradiction met in the raising, or honoring, of the matzah.

By itself, this honoring of bitterness is incomprehensible given the culture's rejection of suffering as a positive value, but in relation to other acts of the evening, this act takes on meaning. The first of the three symbols to be explained is the bone, which is not raised. The symbol of past and future is important to the meaning system, but it is honored only by being considered first, and through its placement on the plate. The bitter herbs are raised just after the matzah is raised and explained, and the matzah's message of "divine affliction" through enduring culture has been repeatedly conveyed. The bitter herbs follow as a similar statement of an afflicted state, but this time the message is carried in a natural form and suggests the impermanence of such affliction, a meaning compatible with the understanding of the transitory nature of the *galut* state of earthly exile in light of the promise of redemption. Taken together, the three key symbols underscore the concepts of the enduring nature of the relationship with God through the white bone of the past and future, the white matzah of enduring culture, and the natural herbs of the temporary, present bitterness.

The words that state that the bitter herbs are eaten (later) "because the Egyptians embittered the lives of our fathers in Egypt . . ." are followed immediately by the phrase that "in each generation, every

Jew must regard himself as though he, personally, were brought out of Egypt." The mythical framework immediately imposes itself on the historical focus, and the bitterness of Egypt is connected immediately with the present. Although the state of Egypt is itself behind the Jew, the experience of Egypt and the experience of the desert—both as a state of transition and as a state, as at Sinai, of divine communication —are to be part of the Jew's experience at the Seder.

The centrality of bitterness and its part in daily life are made personal through the mandatory eating of the bitter herbs. It is important that the herbs be fresh and very pungent, and the rule for their consumption is generally obeyed with a bit of trepidation.

The directions for eating the herbs reinforce the visual message of their participation in all facets of life. They are eaten first in combination with the sweet, natural *haroset,* and later with the matzah that represents the people as a whole, the Israel matzah. Specific directions for each consumption add to the meaning of the act.

Although the Haggadah recommends that participants recline "like free men" throughout the ritual, it insists on it only when they are drinking the wine, eating the matzah after the benediction and the *afikoman,* and eating the matzah and bitter herbs together. Reclining to the left mutes the negative message of the left and emphasizes the right, and so underscores the relation of wine and joy, the positive state of the upper, *kohen* and Levi matzahs, and the relation of the *afikoman* to the focus on redemption of the concluding section of the Haggadah. The celebrant *must not* recline when eating the bitter herbs dipped in *haroset,* an order unique in the Seder. In addition, the *haroset* must not be allowed to mask the bitterness of the herbs, and so must be shaken off. The bitterness of the herbs is therefore heightened in two ways: first, by the mandatory presence of the left hand, and then by contrast with its opposite. The sweet *haroset* is one of the favorite foods of the evening. To dip the bitter herbs in the *haroset* and then discard them is to tease, and thus to refocus attention on the herbs. Through dipping, the bitter herbs, associated earlier in the Seder with the transition from Egypt and the desert, are brought into contact with another representation of impermanence and temporality, this time in sweet form. The bitter and the sweet aspects of earthly existence meet, but the sweet is even more temporary than the bitter, as it is shaken off. There is nothing to hide the bitterness when it is consumed this time, in contrast to the second ceremonial eating that follows. Even if one were to ignore the rule to shake the *haroset* from the bitter herbs and so taste the *haroset* as fully as the herbs, the unusual, mandatory presence of the left hand would introduce the negative message.

When the celebrant eats the herbs with the Israel matzah, he reclines to the left. In placing the herbs between two pieces of the matzah, to make the "Hillel sandwich," the bitterness is "contained" by culture in the form of man's most perfected creation. As the positive right hand raises the matzah, it reinforces the concept of the joy of culture despite its measure of bitterness. The two consecutive eatings of the herbs, therefore, highlight the positive value of culture as an enduring good despite the temporary sensation of bitterness that is experienced.

Where there are two portions of bitter herbs, the whole pieces in the center are eaten with the *haroset*, the grated ones at the bottom of the plate with the matzah. Like the situation of the matzah, this lower position combines right and left, but is weighted instead toward the negative. Eating the lower portion of bitter herbs with the matzah would result in a balance between positive and negative if it were not for the mandatory emphasis of the right hand.

The bitter herbs are eaten after the benedictions that precede the meal, and therefore introduce the present social communion with a double taste of bitterness. With the eggs eaten before the meal, the bitter herbs temper but do not overwhelm the conviviality that comes from the wine, the good food, and the company.

The measures that qualify the joy of the evening through a heightened awareness of the negative aspects of the transitional period—the double portion of bitter herbs, the additional plate of eggs, the *kittel*, and the requirement that the *haroset* be shaken off the bitter herbs— seem to reflect the social climate of the Middle Ages in eastern Europe when these practices were introduced. This was a time of peasant uprisings and other threats to physical and social existence, when ritual forms hardened to ensure compliance with the Law and so hasten the coming of the messiah.

Today, relatively few Seders in America are conducted with a *kittel*, and the frequent omission of eggs at a funeral meal has deprived the plate of eggs of much of its meaning. Many Seder plates indicate the placement of the bitter herbs in the center only; the second, lower position that reinforces the concept of bitterness is eliminated. The very common circular arrangement of the symbols on modern plates locates the bone, egg, *haroset*, and greens in the same place as the traditional arrangement, but the bitter herbs, perhaps for aesthetic reasons, are moved to center left and right, or center top and bottom (figures 7). Whatever the reason for the change in their position, the bitter herbs still combine all poles, right and left, up and down, and so bitterness is still conceptually central. In both cases, as in the older arrangement, that which is not whole is in the negative position, and that which is "completed" is positive. This point should not be overemphasized, since both forms of herbs carry the same message. Still, it is consistent that a culture that strives for completion should, in all these cases, place the whole object, where there is a choice, in the positive position.

The celebrants who are using this balanced plate are likely also to ignore the rule to shake the *haroset* off the herbs and, like many Sephardim, eat a full serving of *haroset* and so somewhat mask the bitterness. Changes such as these accommodate the ritual to present experience and so keep the ancient format alive. How the meanings of the past find their home in the present is the subject of the next chapter.

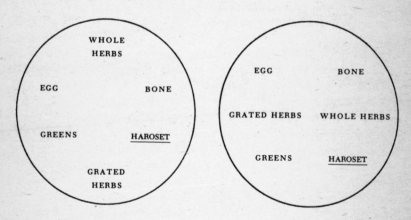

Figure 7.
Modern arrangements of the symbols on the Seder plate.

9
The Paradox Continues

> It is easier to extract Israel from exile than exile from Israel.
> Rabbi Menahem-Mendl of Kotzk

Through the Seder, the Jew gives the diaspora a permanent expression as *galut*. Whereas diaspora implies residence abroad, *galut* is a state of moral and physical exile; whereas existence in the diaspora may be the fault of overwhelming physical powers, *galut* implies laxity on the part of the Jew and some measure of responsibility for his own fate. *Galut* is the covenant, the arrangement between God and the Jew, placed in history. If the mutual agreement of Abraham and Sinai is accepted, then a less than perfect state on earth must be due to omissions on the part of one party or the other. And yet, since God's omniscience cannot be doubted, the experience of daily life leaves the society with many unanswered questions.

The community as created and honored at the Seder is one united in its recognition and acceptance of paradox as its essential bond. The Jew is afflicted because he has been elected; he is placed in historical suspension, fated to reach for a goal of moral perfection denied to man precisely because total perfection is an attribute only of God. This state of suspension is wryly noted in the Yiddish saying "As long as the Jewish exile." Franz Kafka has written: "The Messiah will come only when he is no longer necessary; he will come only on the day after his arrival; he will come, not on the last day, but on the very last" (1958:81).

The Seder stresses hope, man's power to change himself and society, and the shining promise of Jerusalem, but so long as there is the absolute distinction between man and God, the Jew will always be stopped short of his goal. Exile is fundamental to the conceptualization of Jewish community: although he may unite with others through art, intellectual pursuits, or social ideals, the Jew remains one who is defined in the Seder by his separate moral history.

Jewish culture has been devoted to the creation of order through discrimination and opposition, the setting up of mutually exclusive, bounded categories of thought and the elimination, or at least the safe containment, of ambiguity. The inherent logic of the system of thought produces discord on the existential level: when the underlying oppositions are expressed as "Egypt" and "Jerusalem," or "God" and "mankind," or "good" and "evil," the Jew is left with insoluble problems of his own relationship to these concepts. The problem of universality and exclusivity arises when the category "Jew" is both included in "mankind" and also given a particular designation. The ritual tries to relax the tensions generated by the necessary ordering of experience through dichotomy by introducing ambiguities or compromises that are acceptable, and they are acceptable because they are related to a sacred, unknowable, but rational source. The symbolic actions of the ritual engage the community in a game of intellectual *trompe-l'oeil* as they present contradictory experiences of bitter and sweet as divinely ordained and so somehow not mutually exclusive. The symbols can appear to present harmony because they can be the place where disharmonies meet: the matzah can represent both election and affliction, the egg both life and death.

The Seder starts with the premise of God's basic concern and benevolence and displays the group in willing, if demanding, obedience to God. The people of the dispersion have felt free to include reminders to God of his responsibilities as they exhibit theirs, and to include statements about the bitterness of daily life as they also recognize its sweetness. If they express their hope in the future through symbols of joy and confident songs, it is an active hope that is expressed in statements of their own abilities to affect to some extent the outcome of history, as in the communal self-perfection realized at the Seder. This sense of dynamic hope is implicit in the Hebrew word for hope, *tikvah*, the root of which means "tension." This positive tension unites all the polar concepts present at the Seder through symbolic forms that make despair the springboard for hope, and hope the condition of despair. The continual bringing together of contraries—raising the matzah, and the matzah itself, mixing herbs and *haroset*, opposing bread and wine, Elijah—does not erase either pole but allows each to color its opposite. These concepts, implicit in the liturgy throughout the year, can be overlooked in the routines and problems of everyday life. Once a year they are articulated in a form that touches each member of the community and that gives it a perspective to sustain and guide it in the coming year. Each person not only receives the meanings but participates in their creation and dissemination—that is, he participates in the definition and evolution of his culture through the medium of the Seder.

Because the story recalled at the Seder is taken from the Torah given by God, its use at the ritual as an explanatory form for daily experience consecrates at the same time as it gives meaning and purpose to events. The recounting of the mythical history of the passage from slavery to freedom takes place in an atmosphere that engages the mind and emotions and also maximizes the chances of each person's being present. If one is not at the Seder because of the biblical command, one is there because of the good food and wine, the family ties and friendships. The story that unifies Jewish societies through time is presented in the intimacy of the home in a manner that erases the differences that divide individuals and enhances the bonds that unite.

While community ties are being renewed and strengthened through controlled, personal contact, "community" itself is being reaffirmed as an ideal, eternal form, freed from the immediate frames of time and space, and more closely related to God than to the material conditions of existence. This is accomplished in several ways. The prime locus of community contact with God is shifted from the Temple, or synagogue, to the home, where ties are nonrationalized, emotive, sensuous. In this rule-dominated society and ritual, no instructions govern the seating around the table other than the leader's position, and perhaps that of his wife, and the participants gather in a random mixture of ages, sexes, statuses, abilities, occupations, and tribal heritage. The food and wine of the Passover meal relax the participants while they reinforce the ideas and limits of "community." The individual gathering is extended through Haggadah, Hebrew, Aramaic, Elijah, and other symbolic means to other communities and to God. Family group becomes extended kinship group, a relationship dependent on nonrationalized bonds that extend beyond the immediate social context.

The Seder is pervaded with symbols that support the "in-between," *galut* state of the Jew. It takes place at a transitional time in nature, at night—the time of despair before redemption—the "night of watching." Its prime symbol, the guarded matzah, is expressive of the desert state between Egypt and Jerusalem, and the *afikoman*, "exiled" from the table, is a metaphor of the condition of the Jew. The passage between death and life as both physical and moral states is recalled in the egg of the Seder plate, the additional plate of eggs, and the *kittel*, and the ephemerality of life is present in the sweet but decaying wine and *haroset*.

Above all, it is through the symbols of Elijah and the child that the Seder speaks of indeterminacy and transition. Elijah is the link between heaven and earth, between communities separated by space or time, the bridge between hope and despair. Everyone invites the prophet to drink at the Seder; no one is certain he does, as no one is certain on Yom Kippur "who will live and who will die." The child is pure possibility, a state of becoming, and so, in this context, hope. By becoming like children, singing optimistic tunes, relearning and requestioning the story, all the celebrants are united in preparing for the coming of the messiah—but the Seder will always end before he arrives.

One ceremony in particular suggests the ambivalent but optimistic condition of the Seder: the Fast of the First-born. In Judaism, fasts are understood as self-affliction through which one manifests awareness of a state of personal or social crisis. Fasts are decreed on the Day of Atonement, at marriage, on the new moon, during times of personal or national mourning (as for the Temple), after an evil dream (such as one about the destruction of the Torah), and to commemorate the Fast of Esther, the queen in the story of Purim who saved the Jews from massacre. Well before the fall of the Temple, a fast was instituted on the eve of Passover.

To deny a threat is to recognize its possibility in the first place. Although in Exodus, God spares the sons of the Israelites, still the idea exists of their possible destruction and that of the first-born of God. The danger is first acknowledged through the institution and continuation of the Fast, but as God negated the danger in Exodus, so the first-born sons recognize the change of fortune by turning the fast into a joyous feast celebrating the completion of a tractate of the Talmud, the book that is man's conscious attempt to understand and live by God's Torah. Cake and sweet wine confirm the reversal.

The rules that govern rituals such as the Fast of the First-born, the Search for the Leaven, and other preparations for the festival, as well as the Haggadah itself, give the appearance of constancy and eternity to the celebration of Passover, and so unite all groups in all times. However, to treat these rules as eternal is to violate their nature as symbolic constructions, for it is the plasticity inherent in symbolic systems that has allowed the Seder to bend, and so to live, in a variety of environments. Symbols are not fixed entities existing in a static relationship; rather, they are suggesters, indicators of a range of referents operating in the society itself. When, for instance, a first-born son observes the Fast of the First-born according to prescribed practice, but explains his actions as "in memory of the slain Egyptians" (Princeton University, Hillel Newsletter, 1978), he is not "incorrect." He is, instead, reflecting the more ecumenical atmosphere in which he lives and universalizing the concept of suffering and sorrow. And when the Jew from Calcutta refuses to put on his table the "Matzah of Hope" for the Soviet Jews that the Ashkenazic Jew so freely adds to his, he is making a statement or adjustment of meaning, and by this attesting to a perspective of the Exodus story different from that of the eastern European Jew.

Variations such as these are countless. It is the very fluidity in meaning systems as they respond to—and create—the social environment that has allowed the Seder to continue despite the widely different circumstances in which it has been celebrated, from comfortable homes to concentration camps, from the medieval ghetto to the present-day kibbutz. It provides a forum for some of the most essential concerns of Jewish culture in a way that is both portable and open to modification.

The Jews of the concentration camps of Vichy France obviously could not observe all the rules of Passover. Still, they wrote their own abbreviated Haggadah and compared their oppressors to the Egyptians of the Exodus. Similarly, in the ghetto of Warsaw in 1943, the Seder celebrated just before the final uprising and massacre included these lines, which borrow words from the liturgy of the Day of Atonement:

> Passover has come to the Ghetto again.
> The lore-laden words of the Seder are said.
> And the Cup of the Prophet Elijah awaits.
> But the Angel of Death has intruded, instead.
> As always—the German snarls his commands.
> As always—the words sharpened up and precise.
> As always—the fate of more Jews in his hands:
> Who shall live, who shall die, this Passover night.
> But no more will Jews to the slaughter be led.
> The truculent jibes of the Nazis are past.
> And the lintels and doorposts tonight will be red
> With the blood of free Jews who will fight to the last.[1]

1. Binem Heller, translated from the Yiddish by Max Rosenfeld in *Jewish Life* (New York, 1956), pp. 146–47. Quoted in Klein 1973:31.

The Indian Jew omits the cup of wine for Elijah and the opening of the door. Kibbutz Haggadahs add words stressing incorporation into the social body of the kibbutz, and the American Jew may insert readings on freedom by Martin Luther King. This latter addition highlights one of the greatest changes of modern times, the presence of non-Jews at this formerly exclusive ceremony. To some extent, the relaxation of the explicit rule in Exodus against participation by gentiles is expressive of a changed social universe, one in which boundaries between inside and outside communities are blurred through daily interaction in occupations, residence, social organizations, and leisure activities, and through the disregard of food prohibitions.[2] Although the designation "Jew" presumes a distinction no matter how ill-defined, at the Seder that distinction may be muted by presenting the particular values of the Seder as concepts applicable to all peoples.

Widening the physical circle of the Seder by including gentiles corresponds to the widening of the conceptual circle of the Seder. By presenting formerly exclusive concerns of freedom, moral perfection, and peace as universal values, the Jew emerges not as a man isolated from the surrounding population but as one united with others through social ideals. This current practice is but a modern accommodation of the old vision of the Seder and of the culture: the Jews as a "light unto all nations," the medium through which God's moral principles must pass. The presence of non-Jews is supported by the frequent absence of the words, "Pour out Thy wrath upon the nations that know Thee not, . . ." and by the sharing of food and wine.

It is through the role accorded the child at the Seder that the ideals, universal or particular, are made immediate. The Seder is sometimes described as "child-centered," since the child has an important role and a game, and because it is the occasion for instructing the child in the story of the Exodus. Its persistence is then often attributed to its compatibility with the "child-centered" focus of American culture. This may be true in part, but a deeper reason for the popularity of the Seder would appear to be that the concept of "child" in the Seder carries all the positive, hopeful messages of change and perfection through understanding that many Jews, whether religiously observant or not, have sought in their secular involvements with liberal politics, higher educa-

2. It might be argued that it is also indicative of a lack of knowledge of the rules. However, while some groups still follow the biblical injunction, not infrequently persons who are otherwise quite observant of the traditional ritual may participate in a Seder with a gentile.

tion, and social institutions such as the labor union and the public school.[3]

The Seder defines the present as a temporary state and man as a creature responsible for and capable of changing his future. These ideal definitions found their social expression in the great immigration to America at the turn of the century. The immigrants took any jobs, no matter how menial, for they saw such jobs as temporary, not as definitive of their social status. If life was hard, still the promise lay clearly ahead, and America was seen as a land in which each person might make the promise happen. No matter how low a man's current station, education would take his son toward a better future.

Yet a diminished perception of being exclusive does not necessarily mean complete ease in the general society. Exchanging the more articulated guidelines of the past and certain symbolic forms laden with particular meanings for more universal vessels may result in a sense of being cut adrift. As concepts are universalized and "freedom" is no longer so much a subjective moral condition as an objective, physical state applicable to any human being, such symbols lose their cogency and their particular ability to serve as sources of self-definition.

As symbolic play may universalize concepts, so it may serve to particularize them; the movement may go in either direction. The differences between the 1923 and 1974 Haggadahs of the more liberal wing of American Judaism, the Reform movement, illustrates the narrowing of the meanings of symbolic forms. At its inception, the Reform movement stressed Judaism as an ethical system only, one religion among many in America, and adopted practices such as a Sunday sabbath in order to bring its members into accord with the Christian society around them. It was also opposed to the re-establishment of the State of Israel; America was considered a suitable Promised Land. The Reform Haggadah published in 1923 excluded, among other things, the concluding words, "Next year in Jerusalem," the recitation of the Ten Plagues, and the passages starting, "Pour out Thy wrath." It also excluded the specific, second benediction over the matzah, as well as the

3. An example of how the Exodus continues to infuse and ritualize apparently secular experiences took place in Washington, D.C., in 1978, at a rally for the Jews of the Soviet Union. Jews and gentiles assembled across from the White House to hear speakers compare the situation of the Soviet Jews with that of the Israelites in Egypt. Afterward, the children were placed at the head of the procession leading to the Soviet embassy. There, the "messiahs" were to present the Soviets with a petition demanding that they "let our people go." "Pharaoh," however, hardened his heart and refused the petition, and the group at the gate vowed to continue to cry out until their "brothers" were freed.

second eating of the bitter herbs. Instead, the bitter herbs were eaten only with the sweet *haroset,* placed between matzah.

The Haggadah published in 1974 restored all these passages. The introduction states that this Haggadah is a return to "the creative beginnings" and not a revision of the 1923 work (1974:5). In an endeavor to make the meanings lucid to the participants no matter what their background, the sequence of events is changed somewhat and supplementary readings are included.

The differences between the two Reform Haggadahs, the Union Haggadah and the "New Union Haggadah," appear to reflect changes in the practices and comprehension of Judaism within the Reform movement. In the interim between publications, the Reform movement has generally given its support to Zionism and to Israel, has reverted to the Saturday sabbath, and, in some congregations, has allowed formerly prohibited traditional ritual forms such as the head covering and the prayer shawl to be reintroduced at the discretion of the individual. Although certain basic tenets of the Reform movement remain quite distinct from the Conservative and, more particularly, the Orthodox positions, the changes in the Haggadah appear to express the changed perspective of its membership. While still concerned with the universals that unite Jews with other people, the Reform Haggadah also indicates an increased interest in those perspectives that distinguish the Jew and give him his separate identity.

It is the plasticity of symbolic expression that allows the Seder to adapt to different settings and makes it capable of bridging discrepancies between ideology and actuality. Celebrants come to the Seder with an appreciation of the disparity between the utopian promises of the Exodus and the practical reality in which they live. As a formal gathering of society, a ritual will necessarily include the ideological and personal tensions that are part of everyday life, but if that society is to continue—that is, to stay in communication—then a way must be found to keep these disagreements within the family and to keep in motion the social exchange of ideas and actions that binds society.

By presenting paradox as an essential component of the Jew's moral and historical situation, the result of a rational covenant between Israel and God, and by including symbols of resolution, hope, and change, the Seder contains the potentially disruptive power of the community's recognition of its own state of exile. Through the yearly assembly, the Seder exhibits the community's often puzzled trust in God's promise. It temporarily puts aside the problems inherent in the community's election by attributing the apparent paradox of its situation to the limits of man's rational faculties. Still, although placing problems in God's hands for future comprehension may temporarily mitigate the anxiety they produce, as in the saying "When Elijah comes, all unanswered questions will be answered," resolution is merely postponed.

Bibliography

Adler, Rachel. 1973. *Tum'ah* and *toharah:* Ends and beginnings. In *Response: The Jewish woman, an anthology,* edited by Liz Koltun, 7:2, 117–27.

Arendt, Hannah. 1968. *The origins of totalitarianism, part one: Antisemitism.* New York: Harcourt, Brace & World.

Ausubel, Nathan. 1964. *The book of Jewish knowledge.* New York: Crown.

Ausubel, Nathan and Ausubel, Maryann. 1957. *A treasury of Jewish poetry.* New York: Crown.

Ayalti, Hanan. 1949. *Yiddish proverbs.* New York: Schocken.

Binder, A. W. 1971. *Studies in Jewish music.* New York: Bloch.

Birnbaum, Philip. 1975. *A book of Jewish concepts.* New York: Hebrew Publishing Company.

Bronstein, Herbert, ed. 1974. *A Passover Haggadah (The New Union Haggadah).* New York: Central Conference of American Rabbis.

Buber, Martin. 1966. *The origin and meaning of Hasidism.* New York: Harper & Row.

———. 1975. *Tales of the Hasidim: The early masters.* New York: Schocken.

Cassirer, Ernst. 1972. *An essay on man.* New York and London: Yale University Press.

Chill, Abraham. 1974. *The Mitzvot.* Jerusalem: Keter.

Cohen, Jacob. 1970. *The royal table: An outline of the dietary laws of Israel.* Jerusalem and New York: Feldheim.

Donin, Hayim Halevy. 1972. *To be a Jew: A guide to Jewish observances in contemporary life.* New York: Basic Books.

Douglas, Mary. 1970. *Purity and danger.* Middlesex, England: Pelican.

———. 1973. *Natural symbols.* New York: Random House-Vintage Books.

Durkheim, Emile. 1969. *Elementary forms of religious life.* New York: Free Press.

Eliade, Mircea. 1959. *The sacred and the profane.* New York: Harcourt, Brace & World.

el-Zein, Abdul Hamid M. 1974. *The sacred meadows.* Northwestern University Press.

———. 1977. Beyond ideology and theology: The search for the anthropology of Islam. *Annual Review of Anthropology* 6:227–54.

Encyclopedia Judaica Jerusalem. 1971. Haggadah, 7:1079–1103; Passover, 13: 173–83. Jerusalem: Keter.

Epstein, Isidore. 1959. *Judaism*. Baltimore: Penguin.

Feldman, David. 1974. *Marital relations, birth control, and abortion in Jewish law*. New York: Schocken.

Fishman, Isadore. 1976. *Gateway to the Mishnah*. Bridgeport, Conn.: Hartmore House.

Fromm, Erich. 1969. *You shall be as gods*. Greenwich, Conn.: Fawcett.

Gans, H. 1958. The Jews of Park Forest. In *The Jews: Social patterns of an American group*, edited by Marshall Sklare, pp. 205–48. New York: Free Press.

Ganzfried, Solomon. 1961. *Kitzer Shulhan Arukh: Code of Jewish law*, translated by Hyman E. Goldin. New York: Hebrew Publishing Company.

Gaster, Theodor. 1949. *Passover, its history and traditions*. New York: Henry Schuman.

Geertz, Clifford. 1965. Religion as a cultural system. In *Anthropological approaches to the study of religion*, edited by Michael Banton. (Association of social anthropologists monographs, no. 3). London: Tavistock.

———. 1968. Ethos, world view, and the analysis of sacred symbols. *Antioch Review* 17:421–37.

———. 1971. Deep play: Notes on the Balinese cockfight. In *Myth, symbol and culture*, edited by C. Geertz, pp. 1–37. New York: Norton.

———. 1973. Thick description: Toward an interpretive theory of culture. In *The interpretation of cultures*, pp. 3–30. New York: Basic Books.

Glustrom, Simon. 1966. *The language of Judaism*. New York: Jonathan David.

Goodman, Philip. 1961. *The Passover anthology*. Philadelphia: Jewish Publication Society.

Grayzel, Solomon. 1969. *A history of the Jews*. Philadelphia: Jewish Publication Society.

Haggadah for Passover. 1951. New York: Hebrew Publishing Company.

Harris, Monford. 1976. On entering the order of history. *Judaism* 25:2, 167–74.

Heilman, Samuel. 1973. *Synagogue life*. Chicago: University of Chicago Press.

Hertz, Joseph, ed. and trans. 1944. *Sayings of the Fathers*. New York: Behrman House.

———. 1963a. *Daily Prayer Book*. New York: Bloch.

———. 1963b. *Pentateuch and Haftorahs*. London: Soncino.

Hoenig, Sidney. 1969. *Jewish family life: The duty of the woman*. Cleveland, New York and Jerusalem: Spero Foundation.

The Holy Scriptures. 1947. Philadelphia: Jewish Publication Society.

Jewish Encyclopedia. 1909. Passover, 9:548–56. New York and London: Funk and Wagnalls.

Kafka, Franz. 1958. *Parables and paradoxes*. New York: Schocken.

Kahn, Shlomo. 1969. *From twilight to dawn: The traditional Passover Haggadah*. New York: Scribe Publications.

Kaplan, Mordecai; Kohn, Eugene; and Eisenstein, Ira. 1942. *The new Haggadah*. New York: Behrman House.

Kasher, Menahem M. 1950. *Israel Passover Haggadah*. New York: American Biblical Encyclopedia Society.

Kirschenbaum, David. 1968. *Feast days, fast days*. New York: Bloch.

Klausner, Joseph. 1955. *The messianic idea in Israel.* New York: Macmillan.

Klein, Mordell, ed. 1973. *Passover.* Jerusalem: Keter.

Kramer, J. R., and Leventman, Seymour. 1961. *Children of the gilded ghetto.* New Haven: Yale University Press.

Lauterbach, Jacob Z. 1970. *Studies in Jewish law, custom and folklore.* New York: Ktav Publishing Company.

Leach, Edmund. 1968. Ritual. In *International Encyclopedia of the Social Sciences,* 13:520–26.

———. 1971. Two essays concerning the symbolic representation of time. In *Rethinking anthropology,* pp. 124–36. Atlantic Heights, N. J.: Humanities Press.

Levin, Meyer, ed. 1973. *An Israel Haggadah.* New York: Harry Abrams.

Lévi-Strauss, Claude. 1966. The culinary triangle. *Partisan Review* 33:586–95.

———. 1967. *Structural anthropology.* Garden City, New York: Doubleday-Anchor.

———. 1970a. *The raw and the cooked.* New York: Harper and Row.

———. 1970b. *The savage mind.* Chicago: University of Chicago Press.

Lipman, Eugene, ed. 1970. *Mishnah.* New York: Norton.

Loewy, Joseph, and Guens, Joseph. 1928. *Haggadah.* Vienna: Joseph Schlesinger.

Malinowski, Bronislaw. 1954. *Magic, science and religion.* Garden City, N. Y.: Doubleday-Anchor.

Milgrim, Abraham. 1973. *Jewish worship.* Philadelphia: Jewish Publication Society.

Morgenstern, Julian. 1963. *The fire upon the altar.* Leiden: E. J. Brill.

Montefiore, C. G., and Loewe H. 1963. *A rabbinic anthology.* Philadelphia: Jewish Publication Society.

Nahmad, H. M., ed. 1974. *A portion in paradise and other Jewish folktales.* New York: Schocken.

Ortner, Sherry. 1973. On key symbols. *American Anthropologist* 75:5, 1338–46.

———. 1974. Is female to male as nature is to culture? In *Woman, culture and society,* edited by Michelle Zimbalist Rosaldo and Louise Lamphere, pp. 67–87. Stanford: Stanford University Press.

Podwal, Mark. 1972. *Let my people go: A Haggadah.* New York: Darien House.

Ponce, Charles. 1973. *Kabbalah.* Wheaton, Ill.: Theosophical Publishing House.

Princeton University. B'nai Brith Hillel Foundation. *Newsletter,* April 1978.

Rappoport, Angelo. 1937. *The folklore of the Jews.* London: Soncino.

Rosenau, William. 1912. *Jewish ceremonial customs and institutions.* Baltimore: Lord Baltimore Press.

Roth, Cecil, ed. 1959. *The Passover Haggadah.* London: Soncino.

Schauss, Hayyim. 1938. *The Jewish festivals.* New York: Union of American Hebrew Congregations.

Scholem, Gershom. 1941. *Major trends in Jewish mysticism.* New York: Schocken.

———. 1949. *Zohar: The book of splendor.* New York: Schocken.

Siegel, Richard; Strassfeld, Michael; and Strassfeld, Sharon. 1973. *The Jewish catalog.* Philadelphia: Jewish Publication Society.

Silbermann, A. M., ed. 1936. *Die Haggadah des Kindes.* Berlin: Hebraischer Verlag "Menorah" G.m.b.H.

Sklare, Marshall. 1958. *The Jews: Social patterns of an American group.* New York: Free Press.

——. and Joseph Greenblum. 1967. *Jewish identity on the suburban frontier.* New York: Basic Books.

Sperling, Abraham I. 1968. *Reasons for Jewish customs and traditions.* New York: Bloch.

Strassfeld, Sharon and Strassfeld, Michael. 1976. *The second Jewish catalog.* Philadelphia: Jewish Publication Society.

Talmud (Babylonian). 1938. Seder Mo'ed: Tract Pesahim. Translated by I. Epstein. London: Soncino.

Torah. 1962. Philadelphia: Jewish Publication Society.

Trachtenberg, Joshua. 1974. *Jewish magic and superstition.* New York: Atheneum.

Trattner, Ernest T. 1955. *Understanding the Talmud.* New York: Thomas Nelson and Sons.

Turner, Victor. 1968. Myth and symbol. In *International Encyclopedia of the Social Sciences,* 10:576–82.

——. 1970. *The forest of symbols.* Ithaca and London: Cornell University Press.

Union Haggadah. 1923. New York: Central Conference of American Rabbis.

van Gennep, Arnold. 1969. *The rites of passage.* Chicago: University of Chicago Press.

Washburne, Chandler. 1968. Primitive religion and alcohol. *International Journal of Comparative Sociology* 9:2, 97–105.

Weber, Max. 1964. *The sociology of religion.* Boston: Beacon Press.

Wescott, Joan. 1962. The sculpture and myths of Eshu-elegba, the Yoruba trickster. *Africa* 32:336–54.

Wiesel, Elie. 1972. *Souls on fire.* New York: Random House.

——. 1973. *The oath.* New York: Random House.

Yerushalmi, Yosef Hayim. 1975. *Haggadah and history.* Philadelphia: Jewish Publication Society.

Zalman, Rabbi Schneur, of Liadi. 1972. *Likutei Amarim (Tanya),* translated by Nissan Mindel. New York: Kehot Publication Society.

Zohar, n.d. Translated by Maurice Simon and Harry Sperling. New York: Rebecca Bennet Publications.

Index

Intere

452)
berg.
each-
onist
him.
95)

in
this
to
of
ave
hat

95)

ilu-
ish
by
oth
5)

ex-
gh-
ire
5)

T
P

P   ed
a   er
t   sh
o   e.

Name

Address

City_____State_____Zip Code_____

Allow 4-6 weeks for delivery.
This offer is subject to withdrawal without notice.